T0352450

Change in Teaching and Learning

ESTONIAN STUDIES IN EDUCATION

Edited by Jaan Mikk, Marika Veisson and Piret Luik

Volume 5

PETER LANG
EDITION

Jaan Mikk / Marika Veisson / Piret Luik (eds.)

CHANGE IN TEACHING
AND LEARNING

PETER LANG
EDITION

Bibliographic Information published by the Deutsche Nationalbibliothek
The Deutsche Nationalbibliothek lists this publication in the Deutsche Nationalbibliografie; detailed bibliographic data is available in the internet at http://dnb.d-nb.de.

Cover illustration:
Printed with kind permission
of the University of Tartu, Multimedia Center.

European Union
European Social Fund   Investing in your future

Library of Congress Cataloging-in-Publication Data
Change in teaching / Jaan Mikk, Marika Veisson, Piret Luik (eds.).
    pages cm
ISBN 978-3-631-64795-0
1. Educational change—Estonia. 2. Educational innovations—Estonia.
I. Mikk, Jaan, 1939- II. Veisson, Marika. III. Luik, Piret, 1967-
LA850.2.C54 2013
371.2'07—dc23   2013028883

ISSN 1868-744X
ISBN 978-3-631-64795-0 (Print)
E-ISBN 978-3-653-03628-2 (E-Book)
DOI 10.3726/978-3-653-03628-2

© Peter Lang GmbH
Internationaler Verlag der Wissenschaften
Frankfurt am Main 2013
All rights reserved.
Peter Lang Edition is an Imprint of Peter Lang GmbH.

Peter Lang – Frankfurt am Main · Bern · Bruxelles · New York ·
Oxford · Warszawa · Wien

www.peterlang.com

Content

Editorial board

Preface

A new curriculum for compulsory and senior secondary level education has been introduced in Estonia from 2012. The new curriculum is aimed at better integration of the general part of the curriculum and subject curricula. General competencies and topics are thoroughly described in both parts of the curriculum and work with children with special needs is specifically stressed. More attention focuses on the development of research skills in science education and language skills in the humanities. The feasibility of the content of studies and formative evaluation are stressed throughout the new curriculum. Changes in Estonian vocational education have been carried out as well.

The authors of the first paper studied the professional identities of vocational teachers in relation to their new professional roles. The authors of the second paper compared lesson planning by novice and experienced teachers in compulsory schools and found an important difference between these groups of teachers. A longitudinal study of the development of language competence led the authors of the third paper to the conclusion that it is still important to provide students with tasks suited to their cognitive level. The authors of the fourth paper found that the metacognitive learning strategy "summarizing" alone explained 33% of the variation in the PISA 2009 reading results between schools in Estonia. The matriculation exam in mother tongue in Estonia has undergone substantial changes, and the author of the last paper analyses the structure of the argumentation used in examination compositions written by male and female students.

There was considerable interest in publishing articles in this collection. We received 15 proposals; however, not all proposals exhibited the required scientific rigor. Nine manuscripts were submitted and blind reviewed by members of the editorial board and other academics all with PhD qualifications in their field. One reviewer for every paper was from Estonia and the other from abroad. Five papers successfully passed the review and redrafting process and are published in this collection.

We thank language editor Michael Haagensen and his team at Papers Edited and formatting specialist Tiia Ilus for their outstanding work. This collection is published thanks to financial support from the Doctoral School of Educational Sciences (ESF project No 1.2.0401.09-0070), and the institutes of educational sciences at the University of Tartu and Tallinn University.

Diversification of Students and Professional Roles of Vocational Teachers: Teachers' Individual Approaches to Negotiate Work Identities

Meril Ümarik[1], Sirje Rekkor

Tallinn University

Abstract

Several reform policies introduced in vocational education and training as well as diversification amongst students have posed new demands on the work roles of teachers and their instructional approaches. The central question in this article is "How have vocational teachers in Estonia adapted to the new demands and accommodated their professional identities?" The analysis is based on 24 qualitative interviews with teachers from three different vocational fields. Three identity profiles were identified. First, there were "positive change adopters" who had adopted broad work roles and new teaching practices as part of their work identity. Second, "normative change adopters" were teachers who realized the need to modify their teaching practices and widen their work role, but experienced this as something which makes their work more difficult and demands more of their time. Third, there were some teachers who had experienced no changes either related to students or in their teaching practices. We will be arguing that, in addition to the personal characteristics of a teacher, the contextual factors (e.g., the organizational culture at school and that prevailing among professional communities in different vocational fields) influence the change adoption strategies of teachers. Moreover, our findings confirm that collaboration among teachers facilitates sense-making of changes and plays a considerable role in the professional identity reconstruction process.

Keywords: vocational teachers, professional identity, work roles, diversification of students, reforms

Introduction

Vocational teachers worldwide have recently been faced with several changes in their work lives triggered by multiple concurrent educational reform policies (Kirpal, 2011). The change processes in post-communist countries have been particularly rapid and systemic (Grootings, 2009). During the last 15 years several reform policies implemented in vocational education and training

---

1   Address for correspondence: Meril.Umarik@tlu.ee

(thereafter VET) in Estonia have affected teachers' everyday work practices; examples include introduction of the qualification system and implementation of national curricula, reorganization of the network of vocational schools and legalization of new forms of training. Moreover, the general trend recognized in European countries – the diversification of the target groups of vocational programmes – can be considered as a major factor leading to a broadening and redefinition of the roles and competence requirements of vocational teachers (Harris, Simons & Clayton, 2005; Kirpal, 2011) and ultimately redefinition of teachers' work identities (Cort, 2011).

The issue of teachers' professional identities under the change forces has been considered mainly in the context of general education (e.g., Day, 2002; Drake & Sherin, 2006), and studied only very rarely in the context of vocational education (e.g., Vähäsantanen & Eteläpelto, 2009). The central question in this article is how vocational teachers in Estonia have adapted to the changing demands on teachers' work roles resulting from the reform policies as well as diversification of the learners. Moreover, how can the teachers be supported in their identity negotiation and change adoption process?

The analysis of 24 qualitative interviews with VET teachers in Estonia from three different vocational fields demonstrated very different perceptions and change management strategies among vocational teachers.

Teachers' professional identities and working roles

Most authors agree that identity, including professional identity, is not a fixed attribute, but a relational phenomenon. Identity development is an ongoing process of interpreting oneself as a certain kind of person and being recognized as such in a given context (Beijaard, Meijer & Verloop, 2004, p.108). Professional identity refers not only to the influence of the conceptions and expectations of other people, including generally accepted images in society about a teacher's role and knowledge basis, but also to what teachers themselves find important in their professional lives based on their personal backgrounds. Thereby, teachers construct and maintain a sense of professional identity that coheres with their beliefs about teachers' work roles and conceptions of good teaching (O'Connor, 2008, p.118).

A teacher's sense of professional identity manifests itself in their job satisfaction, occupational commitment, self-efficacy and change in the degree of motivation (Canrinus, Helms-Lorenz, Beijaard, Buitink, & Hofman, 2011). However, though identity construction is a complex process characterized by continuous interpretation and reinterpretation of one's experiences and encounters, professional identity is not attributable in a similar fashion to all teachers. Canrinus with her co-authors (2011) provided three distinct identity profiles based on their study of teachers' professional identity profiles: unsatisfied and unmotivated, motivated and affectively committed, and competence doubting. Other studies (Beijaard *et al.*, 2004; Vähäsantanen & Etaläpelto, 2009) have confirmed that teachers differ in the way they deal with professional knowledge and attitudes depending on the value they personally attach to them. Thereby, we can argue that there is no single teaching culture in a school and that every teacher, although being constrained by the context, may construct his or her own teaching culture to a certain extent.

Professional identity is often treated in relation to the issue of how teachers respond to educational changes (e.g., Day, 2002; Drake & Sherin, 2006; Vähäsantanen & Eteläpelto, 2009). Experienced teachers in particular may experience a conflict where there are changes in their immediate work environment (Beijaard *et al.*, 2004). However, the critical factor for sustainable educational change and widespread improvement in teaching and learning is not only to reach the newest teachers who are most open to changes, but also to facilitate change adoption for more experienced teachers (Levine, 2011). In order to adapt to changing requirements, teachers need to make sense of changes on an individual and collective level (Drake & Sherin, 2006; Fullan, 2007). Sense-making is strongly related to identity (re)construction (Louis, 2010, p. 18) and how teachers understand themselves and their professional role. Teachers need to negotiate the new demands on their performance with personal perceptions on teaching roles and teaching conceptions. Some teachers might experience the new demands on their performance as supporting their professional identity, whilst others perceive it as threatening their professional identity (Vähäsantanen & Eteläpelto, 2009).

Teachers' professional learning communities and networks facilitating change adoption

Several studies (e.g., Brouwer, Brekelmans, Nieuwenhuis, & Simons, 2012; Daly, Nienke, Bolivar & Burke, 2010; McLaughlin & Talbert, 1993) have emphasized the role of collaborative professional communities at schools supporting the change adoption. Schools that nurture teachers' professional communities can create resources such as norms promoting innovation, shared objectives and trust which facilitate teachers to change their work. However, as

Levine (2011) argues, we should make a distinction between the concepts of "teachers' professional community" and "professional learning community". The teachers' professional community, comprising shared norms, beliefs and practices that are guiding the work of teachers, may be innovative communities, but they can also reinforce traditional patterns in teaching practices and be resistant to change. "The professional learning community", on the other hand, is "both an ideal type of the teachers' professional community and a related set of strategies for school improvement" (Levine, 2011, p. 33).

The role of the school leader in promoting teachers' collaboration and contributing to the development of the learning culture at school has often been stressed (e.g., Brouwer *et al.*, 2012; Daly *et al.*, 2010; Harris, 2011; Stoll, Bolam, McMahon, Wallace & Thomas, 2006). The idea for promoting learning communities of teachers is that collaboration becomes more than occasional exchanges between teachers; instead, collaboration becomes an expectation, inclusive, genuine and ongoing (Stoll & Seashore Louis, 2007). Teachers working and learning in collaboration tend to possess a wider set of skills, are better informed about their co-workers' work and about student performance and tend to be more satisfied with their professional work as teachers (Daly *et al.*, 2010; Stoll & Seashore Louis, 2007).

In Estonia, the vocational teachers' networks, which have been top-down initiated as part of the national curricula development and implementation process, serve as an important professional learning community – a channel for sharing professional knowledge and supporting teachers in making sense of the changes, as revealed by a recent study on teacher networking (Tafel-Viia, Loogma, Lassur & Roosipõld, 2012).

Radical changes affecting vocational teachers' work in Estonia

After the collapse of the Soviet Union all domains of Estonian society, including education, were pushed into radical change. At the beginning of the 1990s the major trigger for reforming the old (Soviet) dual system of vocational education and training was the need to adapt the VET system with structural changes in society – overall liberalization of society and transformation of the economic system from planned to market economy. This has developed alongside a rapid decline of the industrial and agricultural sectors in the re-independent Estonian economy. Moreover, due to the extensive restructuring and privatization of previously public enterprises, the previous system of practical training was destroyed. All of this posed a major challenge for reforming vocational education and training in Estonia.

In order to accommodate the rapid changes in the Estonian economic system, a new school-based concept of vocational education was developed. Over the last two decades, several reform policies have been implemented in vocational education. The strategic educational priorities in VET reform have involved development of occupational standards and the qualification system, reorganization of the previous network of vocational schools and merger of previously vocational schools into regional vocational training centres, and the development and implementation of national vocational curricula (Loogma, 2004). Moreover, Estonia has been active in implementing EU vocational education and training and lifelong learning policy instruments (Raudsepp, 2010). Starting in the early 2000s, inclusion has been stated as a priority in Estonian vocational education and training (Ministry of Education, 2001). New forms of vocational education and training as vocational education programs for students with special needs and learning difficulties, for school dropouts and those not having basic education (whether young people or adults) has been made a legal requirement. Moreover, continuous vocational training is becoming a central part of the everyday work in VET schools. In the case of declining student numbers and the need to compete for students with senior secondary schools, adult learners have been acknowledged by vocational schools as a way to ensure their economic sustainability. During recent years the number of adult learners has been comparable to those studying initial vocational education programmes. Moreover, even among students studying initial vocational education programmes, the proportion of students aged over 20 has increased and forms almost half (46% in 2011/2012) of the students (Haridus ja Teadusministeerium, 2012). Consequently, teachers of vocational education are faced with several concurrent changes and need to accommodate their teaching practices for divergent groups of learners varying considerably by age and previous education level but also different lifestyles and cultural preferences. Those changes have been accompanied by a worldwide paradigm change in teaching conceptions, a shift from a transmissive to a facilitative approach in teaching (Cort, 2011; Harris *et al.*, 2005). Vocational teachers are expected to facilitate learning and teach students how to learn rather than concentrating on the content of areas of expertise. Moreover, in addition to teaching, teachers are expected to be involved in several development activities (e.g., involvement in curriculum development work groups at national or school level, being part of the student support structure, etc.) The central question of this article is "how have vocational teachers in Estonia adapted to the demands of the broader work roles and accommodated their work identities in that process?"

Method

The following analysis is based on empirical data gathered by semi-structured interviews with 24 vocational teachers from different vocational schools in Estonia. The sample variability was assured by including both men and women in the sample respondents, both Estonian and Russian speakers, teachers from different vocational fields (technical, catering-accommodation-tourism and the creative sector) and from 12 different vocational education and training institutions in different regions of Estonia. As the sample consisted of teachers who had worked in the vocational schools during VET reform in Estonia in order to understand how they have adapted to changes, the teachers interviewed were mostly middle-aged or older. Therefore, the results are not valid when we talk about younger teachers. However, according to the statistics from the Ministry of Education and Research, 63% of VET teachers working in vocational schools are aged 45 or older (Haridus ja Teadusministeerium, 2012).

The interview data analysed forms part of a wider qualitative study on teachers' perceptions of reform policies in vocational education and training in Estonia. The interviews covered four major topics: (1) the general background and career of the teacher; (2) perceptions of educational changes and school innovations in VET; (3) perceptions of curriculum innovations in VET; and (4) attitudes to vocational students and changes in teaching practices. The semi-structured nature of the interview enabled respondents to discuss the topics from their own perspective and raise issues relevant from their point of view. All interviews were conducted by one interviewer, the second author of the article. The interviews were carried out during the period November 2011 to February 2012 and each lasted approximately 45 minutes to 1.5 hours.

The analysis of the verbatim transcribed interviews was inspired by the grounded theory approach. Moreover, investigator triangulation strategy was applied in the data analysis. Firstly, the interview transcripts were close-read and open-coded by both authors of the article. The preliminary codes were discussed with two researchers. Further analysis concentrated on the following key topics: (1) teachers' attitudes towards students; (2) teachers' perceptions of changes in day-to-day work; (3); teaching methods applied; (4) teachers' learning and self-development; and (5) cooperation and networking. Repertoires drawn from the interview data were discussed by two authors. Moreover, a matrix was constructed of the teachers' positions on those five aspects. In presenting the findings, we focused on different repertoires on teachers' roles and teachers' change management strategies. However, we could detect clear connections between repertoires used when talking about students ("weak students", "motivated students", "diverse students") and different work roles. Moreover, the identity profiles outlined ("positive adopters", "normative adopters" and "change-ignoring teachers") were connected with certain repertoires on approaches to teaching as well as more or less active involvement in networking and collaborative learning in the workplace.

Results

Teachers' perceptions of their work roles

Although many teachers experience that the demands on teachers' work roles have been changing, there are different perceptions among teachers in respect to whether a teacher should simply transmit knowledge and skills or be a facilitator of learning and a partner to a student. Moreover, there are different perceptions about whether the teacher's role should be limited to teaching or include supporting students in other respects as well.

1. Teacher as transmitter of knowledge

In spite of the general change in the paradigm of teaching and the shift from "teaching" to "common construction of knowledge" with the teacher's role as a facilitator of learning (Cort, 2011; Harris *et al.*, 2005), a minority of teachers still saw their role as transmitting knowledge and skills. A metalwork teacher describes his method of teaching as follows:

> I show and I explain and the student listens. Discipline before everything... Well, it is one thing to read from the book and quite another thing to tell by heart. If you tell by heart, it is interesting for them [students] and they listen well. But when they don't write down anything, they don't know anything later on. Thereby, I need to force them to write everything I say down. Basically I dictate... (metalwork, male, 68)

The existence of so called "old school" teachers or teachers preferring traditional teaching methods and a teacher-centred approach to learning were pointed out as problematic by some teachers who considered themselves rather as supporters to students:

> I think one of the biggest problems is the gap between the "old school" methods and contemporary students as well as between the contemporary teachers who would like to change the situation. Very many problems arise where there are teachers preferring the "old school" thing that everything should be learned word-by-word without any student interpretations. (hotel & catering, female, 47)

However, the "old school" teachers often used the repertoire of "weak students" to explain their choice of teaching methods. They argued that contemporary vocational students are "weak" and are incapable of either independent learning and reflection or providing arguments. As a consequence they consider methods other than lecturing how things are and showing how things should be made do not work. Many teachers from the technical field told us that e-learning methods, for example, are not applicable for their students due to the lack of capacity for independent learning. To a certain extent the criticism was also targeted towards the educational system and the poor level of education provided in general schools. On the other hand, the poor quality of vocational students can also be explained by the fact that vocational education remains a less prominent educational track in Estonia and many other countries (Kirpal, 2011).

2. Teacher as facilitator of learning and support person

Many of the teachers interviewed recognized the clear role-shift from the teacher as mediator of knowledge to the teacher as facilitator of learning or provider of guidance. It was argued that nowadays when sources of information are varied and increasingly open, as well as students often being more familiar with using different internet sources, teachers have become the background actors. Teachers perceive that in order to motivate contemporary students the old traditional ways of teaching are not enough. Lecturing in front of a class has lost its power and different methods are used:

> I can tell that I have come from being a lecturer to a background actor and a guide. These active methods in learning have changed considerably how we teach and how we guide adults in their work. We carry out some introductory lectures and everything else is done by students and presented by students... (tourism, female, 49)

We can see that in opposition to the repertoire of "weak students" presented previously, here the students are presented as motivated, independent and broad-minded. However, teachers also argued that the level of students tend to vary greatly from year-to-year. In addition to the growing diversity between the study groups the diversity within groups of students is growing in respect of background, age, previously acquired knowledge and skills, but also in respect of the level of motivation. Often the demand from the students is the trigger for a teacher to experiment with new methods.

The "teacher–student partnership" repertoire was repeatedly used in order to reflect the teacher's role in terms of what a teacher gains from the teaching process. This repertoire reflects the general shift from the power of an authoritarian teacher to a more equal relationship between the teacher and the learner. Some of the teachers experienced students becoming more familiar when communicating with them and teachers' rights for dealing with students have diminished. Other teachers enjoyed the more equal partnership with students and considered students as partners they can learn from:

> The authoritarian instruction in our time has changed into teaching that is more respectful towards each other. This partner relationship brings teacher and student closer to each other. There is no looking up, but there is sharing and a vocational school is a place for sharing. … Vocational teaching is not one-way traffic, it is a two-way thing. (tourism, female, 50)

As the technologies change extremely quickly, teachers feel that learning from students returning from internships or from abroad is the perfect way to keep up with developments in their field.

3. Teacher as social worker and psychological councillor

Teachers argued that often the role of guidance is broader than just supporting the learning process. In spite of the fact that during the last decade support structures have been built up at many VET schools aimed at supporting students with social and material problems as well as psychological problems, the teacher's working role involves an increasingly large proportion of work not directly connected with teaching. Teachers perceived that social work is forming an increasingly large part of their workload. This can be explained by the situation of the recent economic decline when vocational education became an increasingly attractive choice for children from less economically secure families and among unemployed adults. Although caring is generally considered an inevitable part of a teacher's work identity, this aspect is leaving less time for dedicating oneself to pedagogical practices as one of the teachers admitted:

> At the moment I feel that I need to be interested in whether he/she has something to eat or drink and whether we manage to buy those cooking clothes. Actually, I don't know whether it is good or bad. But actually it takes a considerably large proportion of my time that I should be using for preparing for class, for giving better feedback...
> (hotel & catering, female, 47)

On the other hand, some teachers felt this element not as something that took up time reserved for other activities but considered it an integral part of their work. Teachers argued that the knowledge provided should not only be considered as the primary focus, but the fact that students manage in their broader life.

> When I didn't have my own group, I didn't know their background. It comes with time. Now when you know their background, you know how to relate them differently or how to guide. To a large extent it is a social work as well as I don't see my mission to educate a good metalworker, but to make sure he gets on his feet in his life. (metalwork, male, 59)

The expansion of the role of teacher is considered as a general path from the novice to the experienced teacher. The same tendency – broadening of the vocational teachers' work roles – has also been observed in other countries (Cort, 2011; Harris *et al.*, 2005; Kirpal, 2011) posing demands on teachers' social-pedagogical and psychological competence in order to work effectively with learners from socially disadvantaged groups or those with learning difficulties.

Teachers' strategies to adapt to changes

As previously seen teachers' perceptions of their work roles are very different. Moreover, in their everyday work teachers often need to deal with different groups of students from different vocational fields as well as from different study levels (e.g., upper-secondary and post-secondary training groups, students studying after simplified curricula, the continuous training programs). In addition to the need to adjust their teaching practices for different study groups, study groups themselves are more and more diverse. Among the teachers interviewed three types of strategies could be identified in responding to the changing demands.

1. Positive change adopters

First, there were teachers who experienced diversity among students as enriching because it pushes teachers into self-development. We have labelled those teachers as "positive change adopters". Teachers experiment with different methods in order to find the right way for each group of students or individual learner.

> The trial-and-error method is used. They are like trial-bunnies for us. ... I really look forward to changes in the education system, as the learners change and they cannot simply be put in front of the desk...We test new methods and say to students... let's try to find the solutions together. If it doesn't work out, let's do it better next time. (tourism, female, 38)

Teachers often regarded students as equal partners and learning as a two-way process. They claimed that students contribute to teachers' professional development in two ways. Firstly, students often have fresh knowledge they bring into schools from internships or international projects. Secondly, the fact that the student contingent is increasingly diversifying by age, background and knowledge challenges teachers into self-development in order to motivate the youngsters with learning difficulties and also interest adult learners. Consequently, teachers experienced their everyday work as a continuous learning process. Teachers felt that teaching both students with lower abilities and the "brighter" ones is pushing them to test with different methods.

2. Normative change adopters

Secondly, there are teachers that recognize the changes in learners and new demands on teachers' work roles, but consider this as something that makes their work more complicated. We have labelled this group of teachers as "normative change adopters" to characterize teachers trying to follow the "norm" of the "right" way of teaching, although experiencing certain conflicts between the expectations of others and their own abilities.

> Students have become diverse. This makes the organization of the classroom practices more difficult. Some are more motivated, others less motivated. Some already have previous work experience from somewhere, others are completely empty sheets. This is a problem as it makes my work more difficult... (hotel & catering, female, 39)

Teachers acknowledged that contemporary students ask for different approaches to the traditional learning methods and a more student-centred approach. However, they admitted that sometimes it is difficult to relinquish some of the control of the class. Teachers also felt some level of emotional breakdown for not being able to fulfil all the roles demanded from them. In contrast to the previous group of teachers, they tried to meet the needs of the students, but experienced testing with different methods and ways of teaching not as fulfilling, but exhausting.

3. Change-ignoring teachers

Thirdly, there was a minority group of teachers who did not acknowledge many changes either in the teachers' work or among vocational students. They argued that "teaching is the same as before" and continued to teach as they had done 10 or 20 years ago:

> Well, it is another thing to teach an adult. He/she doesn't argue against, he/she doesn't say that he/she already knows it. But those teaching methods are still the same, and nothing changes in that, only the facilities are contemporary. But you still communicate the same fundamental principles. (electronics, female, 42)

Among this group there were teachers that were satisfied with their work and kept working in their own "old school" way with little cooperation with other colleagues. However, we could also identify some unmotivated and embittered teachers thinking of retirement. One older metalwork teacher expressed great disappointment in the changing requirements as, according to him, in reality nothing has changed in teaching:

> Nothing has changed in teaching, nothing... Basically, nothing has changed in teaching materials... Technology hasn't changed... I teach the same way I used to... (metalwork, male, 68)

More innovative teachers have also outlined some problems in school between the modern students and "old-school" teachers as well as among teachers themselves. It depends on a school and a vocational field whether the more innovative methods and learner-centred approach are regarded as a norm or traditional ways of teaching are followed. For example, in comparison to the technical fields, teachers from the catering-accommodation-tourism study field tended to express more student-centred views on teaching.

Role of the teachers' learning communities in facilitating change adoption

Some clear connections were identified between teachers' perceptions and change adoption strategies on the one hand, and involvement in professional learning communities or a range of different networks, on the other hand. As a rule, those teachers having positive attitudes towards new challenges at work and testing with different innovative methods tend to be more oriented to self-development and are often networked on the national or on the international level. They take advantage of training opportunities and participate in different cooperation projects with other VET schools in Estonia and abroad. It has been argued that those project and training opportunities contribute to keeping up one's competence basis and provide information on what is going on in other schools, and also have a positive impact on teachers' work motivation as well. Those teachers who are more conservative in their use of active learning methods and innovative approaches tend to be less active in networking. Their collaboration is often limited to cooperating with internship companies and interacting with other teachers at one's own school.

The study also revealed that in certain vocational fields the networking and professional learning communities gathering teachers from different schools and also professionals from the companies are more active than in some other vocational fields. For example, teachers from the catering-accommodation-tourism field tend to be highly networked. The teachers from the technical field tend to be less well networked at the national level and they express more criticism of professional associations in the field. As compared to the teachers from the other two fields, the teachers from the technical field also expressed more conservative attitudes and preferred teacher-centred approaches. In addition to the vocational field, the school context and the prevailing school culture also revealed as important factors in teachers' stories. According to teachers, in some schools every teacher is responsible for his/her self-development and day-to-day work planning, while in other organizations cooperative orientation prevails – professional knowledge is shared daily by colleagues and subjects are taught and assessed cooperatively with several teachers involved.

Training is offered to us all the time. 4–5 days a year we have been supported by the school, but we are looking for possibilities ourselves as well. However, you have really acquired the material when you need to tell it to others. We have a learning organization in our tourism department. As we have high workloads, someone goes outside and we share it between us and discuss. Once a month we have department meetings and sometimes we can learn from those meetings more than in real training-courses... (tourism, female, 50)

In some cases, the small collective may support knowledge sharing between the teachers, in other cases it may mean that a teacher is the only specialist in the field and has no-one to cooperate with inside their school. The school leader's role in designing more or less cooperatively oriented contexts was often stressed. A teacher claimed that their school leader had made a real, positive impact in a relatively short period of time:

> The change I have noticed in our school... When I came to the school, every teacher was an individual personality, individual artist. It was not common to talk about what anyone taught in his/her class. Teachers kept it secret what they taught and what exercises they used... Every master transmitted his secret knowledge. But now, thanks to the systemic work of our school leader, who has tried to get teachers to communicate with each other... (design, female, 41)

On the other hand, there were also examples where teachers admitted that a new school leader had created a negative atmosphere at school, discouraging professional development for or collaborative practices amongst teachers.

Discussion: teachers negotiating their work identities

The study enabled the authors to analyse how teachers have responded to the educational changes and changing demands on their role performance triggered by the diversification amongst vocational students and VET reform policies. As the identity construction process is affected both by how teachers themselves reflect their work roles but also on the expectations of others on their role performance (e.g., those of colleagues and the wider public) (Canrinus *et al.*, 2011), it is a continuous process of negotiation.

The study demonstrated that teachers have responded to changes differently, reflected by their attitudes towards change processes and teaching practices applied in meeting the demands of the diverse student contingent. Three different identity profiles could be identified. The first one — "positive change adopters" — characterizes teachers who have adopted broad work roles and new teaching practices as part of their work identity. Among this group the need to test with new approaches is regarded as offering self-development, motivation and job satisfaction. In the case of this group of teachers no large conflict is detected between their own vision of a teacher's role and that expected by others (colleagues or the wider public). The second identity profile – "normative change adopters" – includes teachers that try to adapt to the new demands. However, among this group of teachers certain conflicts exist between the expectations of others and the teachers' own visions of their role performance. Teachers feel that at certain points in time they are unable to keep up with changes. Third, the "change-ignoring teachers" are teachers who have managed to continue teaching as they used to 10 or 20 years ago. Whether there was a strong conflict between the expectations of others and a teacher's own understanding of their professional role depended on the school context or the vocational field. Among "change-ignoring teachers" there were unmotivated and embittered teachers who were thinking of retirement and tried to continue working in their usual way until their retirement. On the other hand, there were also those teachers who were satisfied with their current work but worked in an "old school" way with little cooperation with others. This isolation from the wider community of vocational teachers had provided them with the freedom to work as they used to.

Thereby, our results confirm those of the previous studies (Canrinus *et al.*, 2011; Vähäsantanen & Eteläpelto, 2009) indicating that teachers are not a uniform group, but include both those who experience educational change as supporting their actual professional identity and also those who consider it as a threat to their identity. Similarly, we could identify in our study teachers that saw changing demands as supporting of their identity as flexible and reflective teachers who adapt their teaching practices according to the needs of the learners. However, there were also teachers with a more rigid identity profile who were not willing to change.

We argue that networks and teachers' learning communities play a considerable role in the professional identity reconstruction process. As previous studies have indicated (e.g., Brouwer *et al.*, 2012; Daly *et al.*, 2010; Levine, 2011; McLaughlin & Talbert, 1993) collaboration among teachers facilitates sense-making and adoption of educational changes. Our study also revealed that "positive change adopters" tended to be better networked and enjoyed the collaborative learning opportunities, while the "change-ignoring teachers" tended to be more individually oriented. In Estonia, the teachers' professional networks have been top-down activated in the context of a national curricula development process. However, these networks are operating at different intensities in different vocational fields as outlined by a recent study (Tafel-Viia *et al.*, 2012) and referred to by our respondents. For example the teachers in the catering-accommodation-tourism field are highly networked and activities within this network are supporting teachers in their identity reconstruction. In some other fields (e.g., technical field), the networks have not been activated so successfully. Moreover, the culture prevailing at the school level has a considerable role in supporting or hindering the change adoption and negotiating one's identity. As several authors (e.g., Brouwer *et al.*, 2012; Daly *et al.*, 2010; Harris, 2011; Stoll *et al.*, 2006) have claimed and our data indicate, the school leaders have a decisive role in both diffusing educational change and creating collaborative learning cultures supporting change adoption among teachers.

The article involves several implications for practice. First, the teachers are the key actors who determine the outcomes of the reform policies implemented in vocational education. By concentrating on the teachers' perceptions of their work roles and change management strategies this article contributes to understanding the meanings which teachers have attributed to the rapid educational changes taking place in vocational education and training in Estonia. Second, it draws our attention to the fact that the changes are perceived as well as adopted differently by the teaching community. This should be taken into consideration when planning and implementing reform policies and designing mechanisms to facilitate change adoption. The concerns of those vocational teachers who perceive the drastic and rapid changes in the field of vocational education as threatening their professional identity should not be ignored. Third, the results of the study inform us on how the process of implementation of educational changes can be facilitated both at the national level, by building up network structures as part of the policy implementation strategy, or at the school level, by providing opportunities and encouraging collaborative learning among teachers. Moreover, the study revealed some important aspects of teachers' personal teaching perceptions that can be beneficial when developing teachers' (continuous) training programmes.

Acknowledgement

This article has been completed within the research project "Fundamental Education Change: vocational teachers as change agencies in the course of VET reforms" funded by the Estonian Science Foundation (ETF 9095).

References

Beijaard, D., Meijer, P. C. & Verloop, N. (2004). Reconsidering research on teachers' professional identity. *Teaching and Teacher Education,* 20 (2), 107–128.

Brouwer, P., Brekelmans, M., Nieuwenhuis, L. & Simons, R.-J. (2012). Communities of practice in the school workplace. *Journal of Educational Administration,* 50 (3), 346–364.

Canrinus, E. T., Helms-Lorenz, M., Beijaard, D., Buitink, J. & Hofman, A. (2011). Profiling teachers' sense of professional identity. *Educational Studies,* 37 (5), 593–608.

Cort, P. (2011). Emerging Roles and Competence Requirements of Teaching and Training Practitioners – A European Perspective. In S. R. Kirpal (Ed.*)* *National Pathways and European Dimensions of Trainers' Professional Development* (pp. 45–62). Frankfurt am Main: Peter Lang.

Daly, A. J., Nienke, M. M., Bolivar, J. M. & Burke, P. (2010). Relationships in reform: the role of teachers' social networks. *Journal of Educational Administration,* 48 (3), 359–391.

Day, C. (2002). School reform and transitions in teacher professionalism and identity. *International Journal of Educational Research,* 37, 677–692.

Drake, C. & Sherin, M. G. (2006). Practicing change: Curriculum adaptation and teacher narrative in the context of mathematics education reform. *Curriculum Inquiry,* 36 (2), 153–187.

Fullan, M. (2007). *The new meaning of educational change, 4th edition.* New York: Teachers College Press.

Grootings, P. (2009). Facilitating Policy-Learning: Active Learning and the Reform of Educational Systems in Transition Countries. Introduction. In R. Maclean & D. Wilson (Eds.) *International Handbook of Education for the Changing World of Work* (pp. 499–512). Springer.

Haridus ja Teadusministeerium (2012). *Kutsehariduse valdkonna statistika põhinäitajad 2011/12. õppeaastal.* Available at: http://www.hm.ee/index.php?048182 (Accessed in December 2012).

Harris, A. (2011). System Improvement through collective capacity building. *Journal of Educational Administration,* 49 (6), 624–636.

Harris, R., Simons, M. & Clayton, B. (2005). Shifting mindsets: The changing work roles of vocational education and training practitioners. Adelaide: Australian National Training Authority. Available at: http://vuir.vu.edu.au/1781/1/Shifting_mindsets.pdf (Accessed in May, 2013).

Kirpal, S. (2011). Emerging Roles and Competence Requirements of Teaching and Training Practitioners – A European perspective. In: S. R. Kirpal (Ed.*)* *National Pathways and European Dimensions of Trainers' Professional Development* (pp. 27–44). Frankfurt am Main: Peter Lang.

Levine, T. H. (2011). Experienced teachers and school reform: Exploring how two different professional communities facilitated and complicated change. *Improving Schools,* 14 (1), 30–47.

Loogma, K. (2004). Töökeskkonnas õppimise tähendus töötajate kohanemisel töömuutustega [The meaning of workplace-learning in the context of labour force adaptation with work changes] (PhD diss.) Tallinn: TPÜ Kirjastus.

Louis, K. S. (2010). Better schools through better knowledge? New understanding, new uncertainty. In: A. Hargraves, A. Lieberman, M. Fullan & D. Hopkins (Eds.) *Second international handbook of educational change* (pp. 3–27). Dordrechd – Heidelberg – London – New York: Springer.

McLaughlin, M. W. & Talbert, J. E. (1993). *Contexts that Matter for Teaching and Learning Strategic Opportunities for Meeting the Nation's Educational Goals.* Stanford: Center for Research on the Context of Secondary School Teaching.

Ministry of Education (2001). *Action plan for developing Estonian VET System in 2001–2004.* Tallinn: Ministry of Education.

Ministry of Education and Research (2005). *Development Plan for the Estonian Vocational Education and Training System 2005–2008.* Available at: http://www.hm.ee/index.php?149743 (accessed in December 2012).

O'Connor, K. E. (2008). "You choose to care": Teachers, emotions and professional identity. *Teaching and Teacher Education*, 24 (1), 117–126

Raudsepp, K. (2010). *A bridge to the future; European policy for vocational education and training 2002–10.* National Policy Report. Estonia: Innove.

Stoll, L., Bolam, R., McMahon, A., Wallace, M. & Thomas, S. (2006). Professional learning communities: a review of the literature. *Journal of Educational Change*, 7 (4), 221–58.

Stoll, L. & Seashore Louis, K. (2007). Professional Learning Communities. Buckingham: Open University Press.

Tafel-Viia, K., Loogma, K., Lassur, S. & Roosipõld, A. (2012). Networks as Agents of Innovation: Teacher Networking in the Context of Vocational and Professional Higher Education Reforms. *Vocations and Learning.* doi: 10.1007/s12186-012-9077-x.

Vähäsantanen, K. & Eteläpelto, A. (2009). Vocational teachers in the face of a major educational reform: individual ways of negotiating professional identities, *Journal of Education and Work,* 22 (1), 15–33.

Novice and Experienced Teachers' Personal Practical Knowledge in Planning Lessons

Anne Okas[a1], Marieke van der Schaaf[b], Edgar Krull[a]

[a]University of Tartu, [b]Utrecht University

Abstract

This study is aimed at investigating Estonian novice and experienced teachers' competencies in lesson planning by using videotaping of lessons and interviewing as data collection tools. Twenty lessons taught by ten novice and ten experienced teachers were videotaped. Before, the teachers participated in a pre-lesson interview. The concept of teachers personal practical knowledge was used as a main framework for analyzing the video recordings and interviews collected for the study. Qualitative content analysis brought out differences between experienced and novice teachers in lesson planning and delivery. Novice teachers focused more on the transmission of knowledge and facts, paying less attention to how students acquire and interpret new knowledge. An analysis of the lesson objectives stated by the teachers allowed grouping them into three categories: the objectives being too vague to assess student achievement; being well-defined but no assessment of their achievement was conducted by the teacher; and being well-defined and their achievement identified by student assessment.

Keywords: novice teachers, experienced teachers, expertise, lesson planning and delivery, lesson objectives, teachers' personal practical knowledge

Introduction

Offering students a good education demands teachers with high expertise. There is a long history of rhetoric concerning the need for well-prepared teachers and the central role that teachers play in student learning (Wilson, 2009). Teaching quality has become a central concern of policymakers and educators. This is also the case in Estonia, revealed as an urgent need for qualified teachers (*Estonian Educational Strategy*, 2012). Despite of a pressing need for qualified teachers in many countries, the notion of teacher professionalism or expertise is not always defined the same way by researchers. Traditionally the term teacher expertise has been perceived in terms of behavior or individual psychological attributes, but nowadays it is much more seen as an integrated concept that incorporates

---

1 Address for correspondence: anneokas@ut.ee

teacher knowledge, skills, and attitudes in context while performing professional tasks (Eraut, 2008; Van der Schaaf & Stokking, 2011).

Shulman points to the complexities of teaching expertise. In teaching there is a need for a deep content specific knowledge as well as for pedagogical skills (Shulman, 1986; Shulman, 1987). This knowledge and skills are probably the best way reflected in the teacher certification requirements of the National Board for Professional Teaching Standards (NBPTS) that has developed professional standards for expert teachers in the areas of early childhood, elementary and secondary school teaching. To validate the teacher certification process, based on these standards, Bond, Smith, Baker, & Hattie (2000) conducted a study that compared identification of expert teachers by applying NBPTS with complex identification procedures drawn from the novice – expert research. Its results confirmed a relatively high reliability of the NBPTS in identifying expert teachers. Many educational professionals and researchers agree that the practice of applying for NBPTS certification in the USA has positive impact on the development of teacher professionalism (Berliner, 2004; Hogan & Rabinowitz, 2009).

For achieving high expertise in teaching practical experience plays a crucial role (Palmer, Stough, Burdenski, & Gonzales, 2005). A relevant component of experience that is acquired in teaching is known as teacher practical knowledge (Meijer, 2011; Meijer, Verloop & Beijaard, 1999). The teacher practical knowledge impacts all teaching activities. The present study focuses on teachers' lesson planning skills as an essential prerequisite to the quality teaching and sees it as evolving practical knowledge in teaching. Without a clear vision of the forthcoming lesson a teacher will be unable to effectively organize the instruction.

The aim of this study is to explore differences of novice and experienced teachers in planning of lessons. Particularly, this study focuses on the quality of stating lesson objectives by teachers for their students as one of many aspects of planning instruction. The research questions are:

(1) What personal practical knowledge do novice and experienced teachers use to plan their lessons when stating lesson objectives?

(2) How do novice and experienced teachers differ in their personal practical knowledge in their planning of lessons?

Teachers' personal practical knowledge as theoretical frame for studying lesson planning

Discussions about teacher professional knowledge and learning are based on a dichotomy between theoretical knowledge, which is often codified in books, and taught and examined in courses of pedagogy, and practical knowledge that is acquired on the job. Professionals constantly learn on the job, because their work entails engagement in a succession of cases, problems and projects (Eraut, 2008).

The notion of teacher practical knowledge

The concept of teachers' personal practical knowledge has been an object of educational sciences during the last two decades (Calderhead, 1996; Fenstermacher, 1994; Meijer *et al.*, 1999; Meijer, Verloop & Beijaard 2002). Fenstermacher was one of the first scholars who investigated teaching in the framework of teachers' practical reasoning. He defined personal practical knowledge as the knowledge that teachers themselves generated as a result of their experiences and their reflection on these experiences (Fenstermacher, 1994). Knowledge that is mainly known and produced by researchers and that can be described as knowledge for teachers is referred to as "formal knowledge". Knowledge that is known and produced by teachers (the knowledge of teachers) is called "practical knowledge" (Meijer *et al*, 1999). Teachers' practical knowledge is personal, which means that each teacher's knowledge is to some extent unique (Meijer, 2011; Meijer *et al.*, 1999).

Personal practical knowledge consists of two types of knowledge: knowledge and beliefs, and interactive cognitions (Meijer *et al.*, 1999). Knowledge and beliefs of teachers are stored in the long-term memory, and they are defined as the frame of reference with which practice is perceived. Inter-active cognitions are related to the actual behavior of teachers and related with short-term memory – these are thoughts when teaching (Schepens, Aelterman & Van Keer, 2007). *Teachers' personal practical knowledge* can be broken at least into six categories (Meijer, 1999): subject matter knowledge, student knowledge, knowledge of student learning and understanding, knowledge of purposes, knowledge of curriculum, and knowledge of instructional techniques.

The categories in *teachers' interactive cognitions* refer to particular contents in teachers' practical knowledge: thoughts about a particular class, individual pupils, pupils in general, pupil learning and understanding, subject matter, curriculum, goals, instructional techniques, teacher – pupil interaction, and process regulation (Meijer, 1999; Meijer *et al.*, 1999; Meijer, Verloop, & Beijaard, 2002). According to Schepens *et al.* (2007) personal practical knowledge of expert teachers is considered to be more focused on relevant aspects of instruction, while novice teachers focus mostly on the content and often on non-essential aspects of teaching.

Personal practical knowledge is based on teacher beliefs (Calderhead, 1996), which may guide teacher behavior in the classroom either deliberately or spontaneously. In a deliberate way beliefs are retrieved or constructed in an effortful manner in a certain context and they are assumed to guide goal formation and behavior. Teacher goals are "mental constructs that describe at various levels of detail what the teachers want to accomplish" (Aguirre & Speer, 2000, p.332). Goals can be conceived as long-range expectations for student learning, which are often part of teachers' lesson plans (Clark & Peterson, 1986) and as short-term mental structures that arise in interaction with events in the classroom (Saxe, 1991).

Due to the unique character of personal practical knowledge, teachers differ in what they know and what they think that works in practice. We assume that it is especially the case when novice and experienced teachers are compared. In this study we were interested what personal practical knowledge do teachers use in lesson planning (such as stating topics of the lessons, setting objectives of the lessons). Based on Meijer's *et al.* (1999) research, we will analyze the manifestations of this knowledge in the light of three categories of teachers' personal practical knowledge: subject matter knowledge, student knowledge, and knowledge of student learning and understanding.

Teaching expertise and planning of instruction

Since the early 1970s, researchers have increasingly been interested in empirical studies and analyses of teachers' skills and knowledge. Reaching expertise in teaching calls for about 10,000 hours of teaching experience (Berliner, 1986; Berliner, 1994, 2001, 2004; Ericsson, 1996). Ericsson and Lehmann (1996) pointed out that the concept of expertise has been extensively researched last decades in the context of experts' talents, experiences and knowledge. Palmer, Stough, Burdenski, and Gonzales (2005) identified in their study teaching experience, teacher social recognition, professional or social group membership, and performance as main indicators of teacher expertise. Additionally, expert teachers have characteristics that make them responsive to student learning and achievement (Palmer *et al*, 2005). Novice – expert studies usually provide insights about the behavior, strategies, techniques and routines expert teachers use. This is for instance depicted in the model of Fuller (1969) that describes gradual changes in beginning teachers concerns taking place along with their extending teaching experience. Compared to novice teachers, expert teachers have more understanding of how and why students succeed (Leinhardt, 1983). Novice teachers often experience difficulties in relating theories taught in pre-service teacher education to teaching practice at schools. Experienced teachers in contrast to novices have, developed through experience a practical knowledge base that underlies their teaching as a personal theory of instruction (Carter, 1990; Meijer, Zantig, & Verloop, 2002).

Teaching is a focused activity that includes planning, delivery, and reflection phase (Krull, 2000; Krull, 2009). This study focuses at the first phase of teaching – planning, which provides basis for effective teaching and student learning (Reiser & Dick, 1996). Therefore, planning is often considered as the most important stage of teaching in which teachers engage in the pre-active phase of teaching consisting in providing structure and purpose for what teachers and students do in the classroom (Tsui, 2003). A good lesson planning requires significant intellectual effort, drawing on practical and theoretical knowledge and experience, and involves a wide range of mental activities, including predicting, guessing, weighing, restructuring, and visualizing (Clark & Yinger, 1979). Tsui (2003) points out main characteristics of planning in which expert and novice teachers differ:

(1)   When planning a lessons, expert teachers exercise more autonomy, while novice teachers' planning is guided by rules and models;
(2)   Expert teachers are much more efficient in lesson planning;
(3)   Expert teachers are much more flexible in planning, and they are ready to make changes to their plans accordingly depending on the context.

Method

Participants

Twenty elementary school (grades 6–9) teachers (18 female and 2 male; ten experienced teachers and ten novice teachers among them) voluntarily participated in the study during two academic years (2010/2011, 2011/2012). The teachers worked at seven Estonian schools. The teachers ranged in years of teaching experience from 1 to 44 years, with a mean of 23 years. The novice teachers had approximately two years of teaching experience and experienced teachers at least ten years. The participating teachers taught a variety of school subjects.

Instrumentation

Differences of novice and experienced teachers in their personal practical knowledge were investigated by means of:
(1) Semi-structured interviews concerning teachers' lesson planning (pre-lesson interviews);
(2) Video recordings of lessons taught by teachers participating in the study.

The interviews were aimed at collecting information about issues concerning preparing the lessons. In all, five questions relating to the lesson planning were asked:

1. *What is the topic of your lesson?*
2. *What are your objectives for the lesson?*
3. *How much time you needed to prepare your lesson? Did it take more or less time than usually?*
4. *What did you think about as you were planning the lesson?*
5. *Were there any difficulties in preparing the lesson?*

The questions were constructed on the basis of questionnaires used in the NBPTS validation study *Construct and Consequential Validity Study* (Bond, Smith, Baker, & Hattie, 2000).

The lesson video recordings were used for assessing the agreement between stated lesson objectives and teachers' activities in the lessons.

Data gathering

In academic year 2010/2011 we conducted a pilot study with two teachers. The aim of the pilot study was finalizing the data collection instruments to be used in the present study. One of the objectives of these activities was avoiding excessive intrusiveness of videotaping and interviewing procedures but also ensuring that the interview questions were clear and easily understood. The participating teachers, after being acquainted with the aims of this study were asked to think about the objectives of their lessons, topics of their lessons, key ideas, and the problems when preparing their lessons. The semi-structured interviews were conducted before videotaping the lessons. In total, 20 lessons were videotaped and 20 interviews were carried out with 20 teachers. The participants were reminded that their anonymity was guaranteed.

Data analysis

The qualitative analysis of (recorded and transcribed) interview data was aimed at describing teachers' thinking on lesson planning, categorizing the stated lesson topics and objectives, and for revealing differences between novice and experienced teachers' personal practical knowledge. For the content analysis, stated lesson topics were divided into two categories (student oriented and subject oriented); stated lesson objectives were divided into three categories (stated too vaguely, stated clearly but not related with assessing their achievement, and stated clearly and their achievement identified by student assessment) in cooperation with two independent experts. Both of them had extensive teaching experience. One of them was an experienced teacher of social sciences. The other was a teacher of sciences. In order to avoid experts' subjectivity, both experts did not work at the same schools with the teachers who participated in the study. The content analysis was carried out in three steps. First, the experts read the statements of the topics and the lesson objectives in the transcribed interviews. Then, they observed the video recordings of the corresponding lessons. And, finally, they assessed the agreement between stated lesson objectives and their implementation as judged on the basis of lesson recordings using the following guide:

1. *The wording of the objective is too general and without a desired outcome. The objective is not linked to the students' skill set and it lacks an outcome, i.e. it was almost impossible to control the achievement of the goal. The goal is so general that it was impossible to assess its achievement.*

2. *Taking into account the study materials, the objectives appeared to be defined and were based on the specifics of the subject matter and the topic of the particular class. It was possible to assess the achievement of objectives, but it was not done.*

3. *Objectives were well defined, and the teacher had made an effort to check the achievement of the objectives and to give students feedback.*

The quality of the agreement was assessed by computing Cohen's kappa for measuring the agreement between two experts who categorized the objectives of the lesson stated by the teachers into three categories. The calculated value of Cohen's kappa (0.86) confirms that the agreement in categorization was good.

Results

It is obvious that in good teaching the statements of the topic, setting of goals and lesson objectives should all focus on student's expected achievements. A teacher has to be aware what should students know, understand, or be able to do in order being capable of planning good lessons.

Stating of the lesson topics

During the interviews teachers were asked about the topics of their lessons. The topics that contained in a defined or in general manner the contents that student should know or achieve, were grouped as student oriented. I.e. their focus was on the student, student's activities and achievements. For example discussion topics for the 9th grade students – *Good communication skills are helpful in managing our lives, Internet-based communication with friends*; or *Chemistry in everyday life – toxic substances in our homes (working in groups)*. The topics that listed content of the certain subject matter to be taught without referring to students were grouped as subject oriented. Examples: *Internal and external structure of reptiles; Wild animals; Islam.*

The majority of teachers (eight of the novice teachers and six of the experienced teachers) stated the topics based on the content of the subject matter and the learning materials on hand. Two novice and four experienced teachers formulated the topics of the lesson focused on the students. Some of the teachers found it very important to teach purposefully that material for which students will later be tested on (*Repetition; Prepare for an exam*).

Stating of the lesson objectives

The analysis of the objectives and video recordings of the lessons was aimed at grouping the objectives (stated by the teachers) into three categories according the following guide: (1) too vague to assess student achievement, (2) well-defined but no assessment foreseen and (3) well-defined and their achievement assessed.

Analysis of lesson objectives showed that one of the ten novice teachers had too general (vague) description of the objective – *broaden students' knowledge about the subject* – not allowing the assessment of its achievement. Nine novice teachers set well defined objectives and three of them made an effort to check the outcome and offered feedback to the students. The experienced teachers were more concrete in defining objectives. In most cases their objectives were well defined, and six of them defined their lesson objectives in terms of practical knowledge of student learning and understanding (type 3 of Meijer's six categories of teachers' practical knowledge). Also they assessed the achievements of the stated goals and provided feedback to their students as could be seen from the video recordings. Examples of well defined objectives: *Student is able to calculate the surface area of a square; Student knows what the main toxic substances of household chemicals are.*

Novice teachers focused more on teaching facts. For example, when the topic was *Estonia's swamps*, the main goal was to memorizing the types of the swamps. In verbalizing the topics and objectives of the lesson they were more subject-oriented (type one of Meijer's categories – subject matter knowledge).

The experienced teachers focused more on development of the students' cognitive skills that enable the students to acquire and interpret new knowledge. Some examples of objectives stated by experienced teachers are: *Development of the comparison skills; Development of the description and analytical skills; Development of critical thinking; Development of basic algorithmic thinking.* Novice teachers also stated objectives (e.g. *development of thinking*, etc.) for promoting students' cognitive skills, but failed to specify these objectives.

Experienced teachers focused also on student's activities that were derived from the prior learning and background knowledge of the students. They also tried to focus student's activities that would enrich their background knowledge. For example, the objective of one mathematics lesson was *to practice calculations from top of the head* (i.e. without using a calculator, pen or paper).

The analysis of interviews revealed that some of the novice teachers had prepared detailed lesson plans. However, their activities as seen in their videotaped lessons focused rather on representing the subject material and less on supporting their students' learning. One of the main weaknesses of novice teachers was that their lesson objectives did not specify their students' learning activities that can be observed or assessed.

The time spent in planning the lesson

The comparison of average time that novice and experienced teachers spent in lesson planning showed that there is a significant difference between these two groups. A novice teacher needed 1 hour and 48 minutes to prepare for the lesson in average. The experienced teachers stated using 55 minutes for planning a lesson in average. The difference in average time needed by these two groups of teachers is statistically significant (t = 2.93; p<0.01). Among the answers of experienced teachers to the question "Did it take more or less time than usually?" was frequently the answer *"as usually"*. More specifically, for the experienced teachers the expression *"as usually"* meant typically *"quickly, as usually"*. For the novice teachers *"as usually"* rather meant *"a lot of time, as usually"*.

Teachers' thoughts during the lesson planning

An analysis of the answers to the fourth question "What did you think about as you planned the lesson?" resulted in the following categories:

• Thoughts about the subject matter, learning materials, exercises:
  – *I would like to finish this theme. The content to be covered is very important because the covered material will be on the next test;*
  – *Some of my lessons have been cancelled which is why I got more material to be covered;*
  – *Gathering and selecting the teaching material for the lesson was time-consuming, in order to enable differentiated study for students of varying skill levels.*

• Thoughts about particular class and teacher – student interaction:
  – *I'm worried about discipline, as this is my first year teaching 7th grade students and they are a bunch of hooligans, the lot of them.*

• Thoughts about goals and objectives:
  – *It seems I need to increase the number of practice-based lessons to better prepare these students for the exam.*

• Thoughts about the curriculum:
  – *Even the minimum requirements of this subject program can be too much for some students;*
  – *If the methods and techniques I've used are not working for a student, I am forced to prepare for him an individual program.*

- Thoughts about the individual students:
  - *I spent time for preparing some complex tasks for a student who goes to the subject Olympiad.*

While planning lessons the novice teachers were having much more subject oriented thoughts than experienced teachers. Also, they focused more on teaching facts. Typical thoughts of the experienced teachers were about students, (for example how to differentiate their learning), objectives, and methods (what he would do to achieve the goal/ what he decides to do with students in order to achieve the objective). Willingness and the competence to develop students' cognitive skills was expressed in setting different goals/objectives such as improving the skill of analysing reading texts, solving tasks, mastering certain algorithms, or solving a math problems. To sum up, while analysing the teachers utterances, it can be seen that experienced teachers' thoughts were oriented towards the students they're going to teach and for whom the lesson is for.

Difficulties in preparing lessons

When talking about difficulties in preparing lessons a main concern of teachers was the lack of time. The interviews show that novice teachers are thinking most frequently about the shortage time in preparing lessons:

- *How can I find the time to prepare for the lesson?*
- *Where do I find the time to prepare properly my lessons?*

Also teachers concerned about lesson materials and technical possibilities:

- *There are difficulties in availability of technical tools in this school;*
- *For this lesson, I had to look for more supplementary material;*
- *There was no practicing material for this topic, so I did it all myself.*

Teachers claimed that there is a need for more classes of exercising, so that the students would be prepared for the exams. It was also noted that in order to develop more persistent knowledge, more repetition of already studied materials is needed. Thoughts about availability of technical means were another issue that teachers were typically concerned when interviewed.

Discussion and conclusions

Valid judgments of a teacher expertise may be based only on observing his or her teaching in the classroom, or observing this it from a videotaped lesson recording (Berliner, 2004). In this study a comparison of the novice and the experienced teachers' replies to interview questions and teaching activities in lessons highlighted many differences in planning skills of these two groups of teachers. Previous research has shown that novice teachers have typically problems with lesson planning (Fullan, 1991; Korthagen, 1999). However, most of the novice teachers in our study stated the lesson objectives very carefully. The interviews revealed that they had developed detailed lesson plans as novices usually do. Yet, as it is well known detailed planning does not always mean that these plans ensure quality teaching, as often the implementation of planned activities is more complicated than it was initially expected. A main concern of these teachers seemed to be a lack of time: novice teachers needed almost two hours to prepare a lesson. Studies by Woodward (2001) of novice teachers point to the comparable time consumption problems in lesson planning. Woodward's explanation is that novice teachers, due to their lack of experience, have too many factors to consider simultaneously as they think about their forthcoming classroom activities with students. Instead, the experienced teachers as they reported in this study spent less time on planning. These teachers have a greater knowledge base of the content, and also they are more experienced in altering lesson designs and employing different teaching strategies when needed.

From the point of view of the quality of teaching, it is important that teachers state appropriately learning goals and translate them into student achievement-based, measurable, and rigorous lesson objectives (Instructional Planning and Delivery, 2011). The novice teachers' formulations of lesson topics and statements of objectives were mostly subject-oriented, instead. The experienced teachers focused more on developing students' cognitive skills that enable them to acquire and interpret new knowledge. So, lesson objectives stated by the experienced teachers paid more attention to the cognitive aspects of learning (e.g. *Development of the comparison skills; Development of the description and analytical skills*). These teachers also tried to focus on learning activities that would enrich students' background knowledge. This orientation in teaching calls for competences that belong to Meijer's (1999) third category of teacher practical knowledge. Six experienced teachers out of ten defined their lesson objectives in terms of the knowledge of student learning and under-standing. Interviewing of the novice teachers' on their lesson planning and inspection of their videotaped lessons show clearly that they focus mainly on presenting the subject content to the students and pay less attention on students' acquisition and interpretation of new knowledge. Most of the lesson objectives stated by the novice teachers did not specify what the students were expected to perform as evidence for confirming that learning took place or for being assessed. When interviewed on planning of lessons novice teachers mostly described their activities as related to subject matter knowledge and student knowledge (1st and 2nd type of personal practical knowledge by Meijer, 1999), while experienced teachers focused mostly on the knowledge of student learning and understanding (3rd type of personal practical knowledge). Also, by the breadth and depth as well as by the structure the manifestations of practical knowledge of experienced teachers' are more advanced and developed than novice teachers. The analysis of recorded lessons revealed that more than half of the experienced teachers assessed students' achievement and gave them feedback in their classes. Schepens *et al.* (2007) have also pointed out that personal practical knowledge of expert teachers is considered to be more complete, while novice teachers focus systematically on the content to be taught and often on irrelevant aspects of teaching. Teachers' personal practical knowledge is a result of their teaching experiences. Experienced teachers have been practicing for years. Novice teachers just do not have this long-term experience.

Though many educational innovations involve using video-recordings for increasing the quality of teaching, the problems with exploiting this approach are mostly seen only from the technical point of view (Tartwijk *et al.*, 2007). Typically, less attention is paid to teachers concerns regarding potential intrusion into their and their students' privacy. It should be taken into account that interviewing of teachers and videotaping of their lessons for collecting evidences on their expertise in teaching are not yet legally required for teacher certification in Estonia. Therefore, when in interpreting the results of this study it should be taken into account that Estonian teachers are mostly not used to interviewing, or to videotaping of their lessons. The majority of teachers who agreed to participate in this study were very apprehensive and skeptical already beforehand. They typically needed for more guidance when asking „*What exactly do you want to know?*" or expressed their dissatisfaction "*This is extra work for me, so what benefit do I get from this?*" Estonian teachers are not used to exposing their teaching in either as live performance or in videotaped way. Though videotaping of lessons is a widely used and acknowledged tool for increasing the quality of teaching, it should be taken into account that teachers' dislike of their lessons being videotaped might impact the findings of this study as well as on conclusions made on their basis.

This study has several other limitations. First of all, it was carried out in a specific context with a relatively small sample of teachers, not representing all Estonian teachers. Besides, teachers participated in this study on voluntarily basis. It cannot be excluded that another sample of Estonian novice and experienced teachers may experience different concerns, formulate differently lesson objectives, and use different strategies for lesson planning depending on the subject to be taught and specific classroom situations. Secondly, we have to point out that expertise in teaching is a complex phenomenon. Though the concept of teachers' personal practical knowledge encompasses a variety of elements in teaching skills it does not represent all facets of good teaching. The notion of teacher personal practical knowledge used in this study is not less multidimensional and only few of its characteristic features were considered in this study.

Finally, future research could focus more on promoting changes in teachers' conceptions of reflecting and assessing their own work. The identification of differences in novice and experienced teachers lesson planning skills is for a small but relevant step towards purposeful promoting of novice teachers' lesson planning capabilities by providing them with opportunities for analyzing their work, and thus supporting their professional development.

Acknowledgements

Our greatest thanks go to the teachers who participated in this study. Many thanks to Professor Paulien Meijer for consultations. Also we would like to express our gratitude for the helpful suggestions for revision by the reviewers.

This study was financed by the EDUKO research program and by the Doctoral School of Educational Sciences funded by the European Structural Fund.

References

Aguirre, J., & Speer, N. M. (2000). Examining the relationship between beliefs and goals in teacher practice. *Journal of Mathematical Behavior, 18*(3), 327–356.

Berliner, D. C. (1986). In pursuit of the expert pedagogue. *Educational Researcher, 15*(7), 5–13.

Berliner, D. C. (1994). Expertise: The wonders of exemplary performance. In J. N. Mangieri & C. Collins Block (Eds.), *Creating powerful thinking in teachers & students* (pp. 141–186). Ft. Worth, TX: Holt, Rinehart & Winston.

Berliner, D. C. (2001). Learning about and learning from expert teachers. *International Journal of Educational Research, 35,* 463–482.

Berliner, D. C. (2004). Expert Teachers: Their Characteristics, Development and Accomplishments. Retrieved from   http://www.sportscoachuk.org/sites/default/files/Berliner-(2004)-Expert-Teachers.pdf

Bond, L., Smith, T., Baker, W. K. & Hattie, J. A. (2000). The certification system of the National Board for Professional Teaching Standards: A construct and consequental validity study. Greensboro, NC: Center for Educational Research and Evaluation, University of North Carolina.

Calderhead, J. (1996). Teachers: beliefs and knowledge. In D. C. Berliner & R. C. Calfee (Eds.), *Handbook of Educational Psychology* (pp. 709–725). New York: MacMillan.

Carter, K. (1990). Teachers' Knowledge and Learning to Teach. In W. R. Houston (Ed.), *Handbook of Research on Teacher Education* (pp. 291–310). New York: MacMillan.

Clark, C. M. & Yinger, R. J. (1979). Teachers' thinking. In P. L. Peterson & H. J. Walberg (Eds.), *Research on Teaching: concepts, findings, and implications* (pp. 231–263). Berkeley, CA: McCutchan.

Clark, C. M., & Peterson, P. L. (1986). Teachers' thought processes. In M. C. Wittrock (Ed.), *Handbook of research on teaching, 3rd ed.* (pp. 255–296). New York: Macmillan.

Eraut, M. (2008). *Developing Professional Knowledge and Competence.* New York: Routledge Falmer, Taylor & Francis Group, Inc.

Ericsson, K. A. (Ed.). (1996). *The Road to Excellence. The Acquisition of Expert Performance in the Arts and Sciences, Sports and Games.* New Jersey: Lawrence Erlbaum Associates, Inc.

Ericsson, K. A., & Lehmann, A. C. (1996). Expert and exceptional performance: Evidence of maximal adaptations to task constraints. *Annual Review of Psychology, 47,* 273–305.

Estonian Education Strategy 2012–2020: The Five Challenges of Estonian Education (Draft). (2011). Tallinn, Estonian Cooperation Assembly. Retrieved from http://www.elu5x.ee/public/Haridusstrateegia_ENG_spreads_appendix.pdf

Fenstermacher, G. D. (1994). The knower and known: The nature of knowledge in research on teaching. *Review of Research on Teaching, 20,* 3–56.

Fullan, M. (1991). *The New Meaning of Educational Change.* New York: Teachers College Press.

Fuller, F. (1969). Concerns of teachers: A developmental conceptualization. *American Educational Research Journal, 6,* 207–226.

Hogan, T., & Rabinowitz, M. (2009). Teacher expertise and the development of a problem representation. *Educational Psychology, 29*(2), 153–169.

Instructional Planning and Delivery. (2011). *Teach for America.* Retrieved from http://www.teachingasleadership.org/sites/default/files/Related-Readings/IPD_2011.pdf

Korthagen, F. (1999). Linking Reflection and Technical Competence: The Logbook as an Instrument in Teacher Education. *European Journal of Teacher Education, 22*, 191–207.

Krull, E. (2000). *Pedagoogilise psühholoogia käsiraamat* (Handbook of Educational psychology). Tartu: Tartu Ülikooli Kirjastus. (In Est.)

Krull, E. (2009). Normaalkoolid: kas anakronism või õpetajakoolituse tulevik (Finnish normal schools: anachronism or future of teacher education). *Akadeemia, 21*(3), 524–547.

Leinhardt, G. (1983). Novice and expert knowledge of individual student's achievement. *Educational Psychology, 18*(3), 165–179.

Meijer, P. (1999). *Teachers' practical knowledge. Teaching reading comprehension in secondary education.* (Doctoral Dissertation). Leiden University, The Netherlands.

Meijer, P. C. (2011, October). *Teachers' practical knowledge as part of teacher education.* Paper presented at the Teacher Education Seminar, University of Tartu, Estonia.

Meijer, P. C., Verloop, N., & Beijaard, D. (1999). Exploring language teachers' practical knowledge about teaching reading comprehension. *Teaching and Teacher Education, 15*(1), 59–84.

Meijer, P. C., Verloop, N., Beijaard, D. (2002). Multi–Method Triangulation in a Qualitative Study on Teachers' Practical Knowledge: An Attempt to Increase Internal Validity. Kluweer Academic Publichers: *Quality and Quantity, 36*, 145–167.

Meijer, P. C., Zanting, A., Verloop, N. (2002). How can student teachers' elicit experienced teachers' practical knowledge? Tools, suggestions and significance. *Journal of Teacher Education, 53*(5), 406–419.

Palmer, D. J., Stough, L. M., Burdenski, T. K., & Gonzales, M. (2005). Identifying teacher expertise: An examination of researchers' decision making. *Educational Psychologist, 40*(1), 13–25.

Reiser, R. A., & Dick, W. (1996). *Instructional planning: A guide for teachers.* Boston: Allyn & Bacon.

Saxe, G. B. (1991). *Culture and cognitive development: Studies in mathematical understandings.* New York, Hillsdale: Lawrence Erlbaum.

Schepens, A., Aelterman, A.,Van Keer, H. (2007). Studying learning processes of student teachers with stimulated recall interviews through changes in interactive cognitions. *Teaching and Teacher Education, 23*, 457–472.

Shulman, L. S. (1986). Those who understand: Knowledge growth in teaching. *Educational Researcher, 15*, 4–14.

Shulman, L. S. (1987). Knowledge and teaching. Foundations of the new reform. *Harvard Educational Review, 57*(1), 1–22.

Tsui, A. B. M. (2003). Understanding Expertise in Teaching: Case Studies of Second Language Teachers. Case Studies of Second Language Teachers. Chapter 3: Characteristics of Novice and Expert Teachers. United Kingdom: Cambridge University Press, 22–41.

Van der Schaaf, M. F., & Stokking, K. M. (2011). Construct Validation of Content Standards for Teaching. *Scandinavian Journal of Education Research, 55*(3), 273–289.

Van Tartwijk, J., Driessen, E., van der Vleuten, C., Stokking, K. (2007). Factors influencing the Successful Introduction of Portfolios. *Quality in Higher Education, 13*(1), 69.

Wilson, S. M. (2008). Measuring Teacher Quality for Professional Entry. In Gitomer, D.H (Ed.), *Measurement Issues and Assessment for Teaching Quality* (pp. 8–29). Sage Publications.

Woodward, T. (2001). *Planning lessons and courses: designing sequences of work for the language classroom.* United Kingdom: Cambridge University Press.

Longitudinal Study of the Development of Language Competence among Estonian 4th and 5th Grade Students

Krista Uibu[1], Kristiina Tropp

University of Tartu, Estonia

Abstract

In order to achieve high competence in languages students have to comprehend texts, grasp the meanings of words and obtain grammar knowledge. The scope of the current research is the development of language competence in mother tongue among 4th and 5th grade students. Six hundred and sixty-eight students completed the language competence tests. Results showed higher scores in reading and grammar tasks in Grade 5 than in Grade 4, with girls performing better than boys. In addition, moderate correlations were found between reading comprehension at different cognitive levels and semantic awareness in both grades. Different profiles of language competence, and their stability and change over time were analyzed using a person-oriented approach. The language competence of many students increased, but there were students whose results decreased in Grade 5. However, extreme changes from low language competence profiles to high, or vice versa, were rare. To promote language competence in students it is essential to provide them with tasks suited to their cognitive level.

Keywords: language competence, primary school, gender differences, person-oriented approach, longitudinal study

Introduction

The acquisition of language competence in mother tongue is the foundation of student progress in all subjects. According to Krashen (1982), *language competence* is not the tacit knowledge of the native speaker, but rather conscious knowledge; that is, cognitive control over language structures and conventional use of grammar patterns (cf. Chomsky, 1964, Lenneberg, 1967). Language competence comprises several categories and levels; for example, reading comprehension, vocabulary knowledge, grammar skills, etcetera (Saxton, 2010).

Many researches have focused on reading comprehension and related factors such as vocabulary size and word recognition (Bast & Reitsma, 1998; Cain &

---

1   Address for correspondence: krista.uibu@ut.ee

Oakhill, 2011), verbal fluency and spelling (Echols, West, Stanovich, & Zehr, 1996; Pečjak, Podlesek, & Pirc, 2011), and semantic awareness (Eason *et al.*, 2012). Some researchers have found that there is a reciprocal causation between reading comprehension and grammar skills (Foorman, 2006; Echols *et al.*, 1996). Other studies have shown that such metalinguistic skills as word recognition and spelling are a prerequisite for general language development (Bast & Reitsma, 1998).

The investigation of student language competence, including reading comprehension, has been important in Estonia in recent decades. There have been studies that endorse the results of the official academic language tests in relation to gender differences (Sinka, 2008; Vardja, 2006). Recently, there has also been growing interest in student reading habits (Puksand, 2012), reading difficulties (Soodla, 2010), and problems in Estonian orthography (Uusen & Müürsepp, 2010). However, the comprehensive studies of student language competence, especially in the higher grades of primary education (among Grades 4 to 6), are limited.

The aim of the current longitudinal study is to examine language competence in mother tongue in fourth and fifth graders, including reading comprehension at different cognitive levels, semantic awareness and grammar knowledge. Besides general trends, particular groups of students with different profiles of language competence and changes to that competence over a single year were investigated.

Factors influencing student language competence

Language competence rests on cognitive processes, individual peculiarities as well as student age and gender (Bast & Reitsma, 1998; Cain & Oakhill, 2011). Different cognitive abilities (e.g. attention, memorizing) are needed for mechanical reading and vocabulary acquisition (Skehan, 2008). Higher-order cognitive competences (e.g. information processing, extrapolation) are additionally required for reading comprehension and conventional use of grammar patterns (Krashen, 1982). Students whose cognitive abilities are more advanced generally achieve better results in reading and writing (Gleason & Rathner, 2009; Lenneberg, 1967; Siegler, 2005). Conversely, the lack of a basic knowledge in phonology, vocabulary, morphology, and syntax during critical periods of language acquisition (age 5 to puberty) impedes the development of language skills (Lenneberg, 1967; Saxton, 2010).

Correlations between text comprehension and interpretation, word recognition and vocabulary size have been indicated (Gleason & Rathner, 2009; Connor & Al'Otaiba, 2008; Eason *et al.*, 2012). Written texts tend to be more complex and include unfamiliar words for students (Cain & Oakhill, 2011). In addition, vocabulary items in written texts may vary in their meanings and nuances, depending on the context. As earlier studies have shown, it is quite a complicated task for younger students to reflect on what they already know in order to make connections with new concepts (Siegler, 2005). To facilitate the comprehension of texts, linking new words and phrases with previous content is suggested (Gee, 2012).

When students get older (in the range from 9 to 14 years), reading becomes more significant in order to acquire knowledge (Gleason & Rathner, 2009). Growth in verbal skills (e.g. decoding ability, word recognition) is of importance (e.g. Echols *et al.*, 1996; Pečjak *et al.*, 2011) because incomplete semantic knowledge inhibits the comprehension of texts (Gleason & Rathner, 2009). However, vocabulary as an unconstrained skill is learned slowly (Cain & Oakhill, 2011). Therefore, different comprehension strategies (e.g. monitoring of comprehension, question answering, multiple-choice tasks) have been suggested (Connor & Al'Otaiba, 2008; Krashen, 1982; Rodriguez, 2005).

Moreover, reading is related to grammar because both reading and writing are influenced by metalinguistic skills. Namely, the grapheme-phoneme correspondence rules that must be learned in order to read a text are the same rules that must be acquired in order to spell conventionally (Gleason & Rathner, 2009; Saxton, 2010). However, the acquisition of grammar is difficult for primary school students because grammatical principles and patterns are rather complicated and presumes productive thinking skills: (re)construction, elaboration and deep information processing (Siegler, 2005). Otherwise, students may confront difficulties in spelling and reading comprehension (Gee, 2012; Siegler, 2004).

The present study

In Estonia, student language competence in mother tongue is measured using official academic language tests in Grades 3 and 6. According to the Estonian language syllabus (Põhikooli riiklik õppekava, 2011), by the end of Grade 6 students have to have obtained basic literacy-related skills: reading comprehension and word recognition, knowledge of orthography and morphology, etcetera. In addition, the main rules of Estonian grammar should be obtained to promote writing skills. However, the results of earlier surveys have indicated that student language skills have worsened over the years (Sinka, 2008; Vardja, 2006). Due to its complexity, many students have had problems in Estonian spelling (Uusen & Müürsepp, 2010). Moreover, boys have shown constantly lower results than girls in reading comprehension as well as in grammar tasks (Sinka, 2008; Uusen & Müürsepp, 2010). The reason for this may lie in the fact that students have a deficit in psycholinguistic abilities and metacognitive skills (Saxton, 2010; Skehan, 2008).

Aims and hypotheses

The aim of the current longitudinal study is to examine language competence in mother tongue among 4th and 5th grade students and their progress over time. We assessed student development in reading comprehension at different cognitive levels, semantic awareness and grammar knowledge. The following four goals were set for the study.

1. *To describe the differences between student language competence in mother tongue in two consecutive years.* Language competence rests on different cognitive processes, and their growth over time has been identified (Cain & Oakhill, 2011; Eason *et al.*, 2012; Saxton, 2010). In accordance with student cognitive development we expected to find differences in their language skills. Students in Grade 5 were expected to present higher levels of competence in both easier and more complex reading tasks and in vocabulary and grammar knowledge when compared to their results in Grade 4.

2. *To analyze to what extent language competence in mother tongue varies for boys and girls over a one-year period.* Gender differences in language skills have been investigated in several studies (Logan & Johnston, 2010; Sinka, 2008). Some of them have found that girls outperformed boys in reading and linguistic skills (Cain & Oakhill, 2011; Uibu & Tropp, 2012). Less is known about the gap in the performance of boys and girls over time. We expected girls' results in reading comprehension tasks, semantic awareness, and grammar knowledge to be higher than for boys in Grade 5 compared to Grade 4.

3. *To determine the relationships between student language skills and how they change from Grade 4 to Grade 5.* The reciprocal causation between student reading comprehension, vocabulary and different language skills has been identified (Cain & Oakhill, 2011; Eason *et al.*, 2012). It was detected that

students with stronger vocabulary knowledge comprehend texts better at different cognitive levels (Connor & Al'Otaiba, 2008). The correlations among student reading comprehension, vocabulary and grammar knowledge were expected to be significant, the strongest of them between semantic awareness and reading comprehension.

4. *To examine different profiles of language competence and their stability or change over a year.* We expected the students to have different language competence profiles in Grades 4 and 5, with considerable structural stability of profiles in Grades 4 and 5. Typically the stability of the profile was expected at the individual level, but also some significantly frequent or atypical changes were of interest.

Methods

Sample and procedure

This study is part of a larger research project. Six hundred and sixty-eight primary school students from 47 classes in 28 Estonian schools participated in the longitudinal study. The sample was formed to include as much variety in the students as possible. Schools and classes were chosen considering regions (rural and urban areas), school types (basic and secondary schools) and class sizes (smaller and larger classes). All students studied in regular classes according to the Estonian National Curriculum for Basic School and Upper Secondary School (Põhikooli ja gümnaasiumi, 2007). However, different teaching methods were represented in the participating schools (e.g., traditional teaching methodology, Step by Step Programs).

The students were assessed at the beginning of Grades 4 and 5. Seven hundred and ninety-one students (49.7% boys, 50.3% girls) completed the language test in Grade 4. The students' average age was 10.00 years, SD = .36. Seven hundred and eighty-three students (49.6% boys, 50.4% girls) filled out the language test in Grade 5. The students' average age was 10.98 years, SD = .36. As several students did not complete language competence tests at both measurement points, the number of students included into the final analyses was smaller (N = 668, 48.9% boys, 51.1% girls).

The language tests were taken to the schools by the first author as well as fellow authors of the study. Both the tests for Grades 4 and 5 were administered by class teachers during language lessons; the completion of the tests took approximately 45 minutes.

Measures

Language competence tests (LCT) were carried out to identify the language competence of the students in their mother tongue, including reading comprehension, semantic awareness and grammar knowledge. The LCTs for Grades 4 and 5 were designed by the first author of the article, taking into account the categories in a revised version of Bloom's hierarchical taxonomy (Krathwohl, 2002), the standards of the Estonian language syllabus and official academic placement tests (Põhikooli ja gümnaasiumi, 2007; Sinka, 2008).

The test for the 4th graders comprised a total of six tasks (maximum score 24). To examine the students' ability to comprehend and interpret the information in a text, two reading tasks at different cognitive levels were designed. The first reading task focused on memorizing and finding information in the text. Students were asked to read out the text (in fable genre, 121 words in length) and tick true sentences (*True/ false sentences*, max = 8). In the second reading task students' ability to incorporate and translate information was of importance. Students had to make correct sentences from two appropriate clauses, considering the text (*Comprehension reading*, max = 6).

Student semantic awareness was tested using vocabulary tasks. Students were asked to choose words with correct meanings from a multiple-choice list selected from the text (*Vocabulary*, max = 5). The list enclosed words with equal meanings as well as incorrect words and phrases. Basic knowledge of orthography was assessed using *spelling* tasks. Students were provided with a pool of words and asked to select only the misspelt words (three from 10, max = 3).

The same categories of tasks were designed for the 5th grade LCT. However, the tasks for Grade 5 were more sophisticated than in Grade 4; for example, an extra strophe was added to the fable (185 words in length); more sentences or clauses were involved in the reading tasks (max = 11 for the *True/false sentences*; max = 7 for the *Comprehension reading*). The *vocabulary* task comprised more words in Grade 5 than in Grade 4 (max = 10) and pool for the *spelling* task included a total of 16 items (max = 6). The maximum score in the Grade 5 language test was 34, calculated by only taking into account correct answers.

An exploratory factor analysis (principal components method) using Varimax rotation was conducted for 22 items in the Grade 4 language test. Six subscales with eigenvalues greater than 1 were identified. As difficulties were faced in giving meaningful names to the scales, in accordance with theoretical assumptions, a four-factor solution was subsequently tested. First, four items were eliminated, because they had high loadings on more than one subscale or their loadings were less than .30 on each scale. Then, a four-factor solution was tested for the Grade 5 test, using the same items that loaded to the subscales in Grade 4. One item, which measured vocabulary skills, was eliminated because its loadings were less than .30. The final factor analysis was run for all remaining 17 overlapping items in both grades. Altogether, 48.87% of the variance was explained by variables in Grade 4 and 49.97% by those in Grade 5. Consequently, four scales were revealed for the LCTs: *Higher-level text comprehension* (HC, 5 items), *Lower level text comprehension* (LC, 5 items), *Semantic awareness* (SA, 4 items), and *Grammar knowledge* (G, 3 items). The factor loadings for the items on the scales and their internal consistencies are summarized in Appendix 1.

Data analysis

Both variable- and person-oriented approaches to the data analysis were employed to provide more comprehensive information. First, variable level analyses were carried out using SPSS Statistics, version 20.0. The repeated measures analysis of variance (ANOVA) was used to discover the differences in student performance in LCTs according to two measurement points and gender groups. To report the statistical significance of the group differences in the measured variables, in addition to p-values, Cohen's proposed guidelines were used to interpret the effect size of the partial η^2 (further: η^2) (see Cohen, Manion & Morrison, 2007). The Pearson correlation coefficient was used to find statistically significant correlations between the tasks in the LCTs.

Second, taking the person-oriented perspective, the LICUR procedure was conducted (Bergman, Magnusson, & El Khouri, 2003). From the SLEIPNER analysis package, the version 2.1 module CLUSTER (Ward's method) was employed to cluster subjects according to standardized scores of four variables. In studying structural stability, two sets of cluster centroids from Grade 4 and Grade 5 were compared using the CENTROID method in SLEIPNER. The Average Squared Euclidian Distance (ASED) between cluster pairs smaller than 1 is considered to show good structural stability.

Exact cell-wise analyses of a contingency table (EXACON, χ^2 test) were conducted to reveal different *types* and *antitypes* in developmental trajectories. *Types* refer to trajectories which were observed significantly more frequently than would have been expected by chance, and *antitypes* to trajectories that were observed significantly less frequently than would have been expected by chance.

Results

Reading comprehension, semantic awareness and grammar knowledge

To examine the reading comprehension abilities of the students at different cognitive levels (LC, HC), and levels of semantic awareness (SA) and grammar knowledge (G), we compared the groups means using four task scores. The means and standard deviations of language competence tasks in Grades 4 and 5 for the whole sample and gender groups are provided in Table 1.

Table 1:   *Descriptive statistics of language competence tasks*

	Whole sample (N = 668)				Boys (N = 327)				Girls (N = 341)			
	Grade 4		Grade 5		Grade 4		Grade 5		Grade 4		Grade 5	
Language competence tasks	*M*	*SD*	*M*	*SD*	*M*	*SD*	*M*	*SD*	*M*	*SD*	*M*	*SD*
Higher-level text comprehension	3.26	1.63	3.88	1.48	3.06	1.70	3.67	1.56	3.45	1.54	4.09	1.37
Lower level text comprehension	4.29	1.04	4.45	.98	4.21	1.06	4.35	1.09	4.37	1.03	4.55	.84
Semantic awareness	3.04	1.29	2.96	1.16	2.75	1.36	2.75	1.21	3.32	1.16	3.16	1.07
Grammar knowledge	1.17	1.06	1.34	1.11	1.06	1.05	1.16	1.06	1.29	1.05	1.51	1.13

To investigate changes in student language skills and the extent to which gender related to student results in Grades 4 and 5, we implemented 2 (time) × 2 (gender) repeated measures ANOVA. In the analysis of HC, the main effects of time were $F(1, 666) = 88.48, p < .001, \eta^2 = .12$ and of gender were $F(1, 666) = 16.16, p < .001, \eta^2 = .02$. In the case of LC, the analogous effects of time were $F(1, 666) = 11.72, p = .001, \eta^2 = .02$, and gender were $F(1, 666) = 7.91, p = .005, \eta^2 = .01$. The effect of time was $F(1, 666) = 10.52, p = .001, \eta^2 = .02$, and gender, $F(1, 666) = 19.03, p < .001, \eta^2 = .03$, for the G task. In the analysis of SA, an effect of gender arose as follows: $F(1, 666) = 36.71, p < .001, \eta^2 = .05$, but no effect of time p = .07. The repeated measures ANOVA separately for girls showed a significant decrease in the SA score in Grade 5, when compared to Grade 4 as follows: $F(1,340) = 7.21$, $p < .01$, $\eta^2 = .02$. According to the results, no statistically significant interactions among gender and time were revealed for language skills. Therefore, the students had significantly higher average scores in almost all subtests (except SA) in Grade 5, when compared to Grade 4. Moreover, girls outperformed boys in all subtests in both grades.

Next, correlations between student reading comprehension at different cognitive levels, semantic awareness and grammar knowledge were analyzed. The findings are presented in Table 2.

Table 2: *Correlations between student language skills in Grades 4 and 5*

	Grade 4				Grade 5		
Grade 4	1	2	3	4	5	6	7
1 *Lower level text comprehension*							
2 *Semantic Awareness*	.35**						
3 *Higher-level text comprehension*	.27**	.41**					
4 *Grammar knowledge*	.15**	.29**	.33**				
Grade 5							
5 *Lower level text comprehension*	.32**	.30**	.22**	.13*			
6 *Semantic Awareness*	.35**	.55**	.37**	.22**	.44**		
7 *Higher-level text comprehension*	.33**	.38**	.40**	.20**	.40**	.45**	
8 *Grammar knowledge*	.14**	.26**	.20**	.31**	.19**	.28**	.26**

Note: *$p < .01$, **$p < .001$

The results indicated that there were statistically significant correlations between all subtests for both measurement points; however, the correlations were rather moderate. Of note are the following significant moderate correlations ($r \geq .35$) at p-level $< .001$ (see Cohen et al., 2007).

SA in Grade 4 moderately correlated to HC as well as LC in Grade 4. Analogous correlations were found for Grade 5: SA related to both reading tasks. In addition, significant moderate correlations were found for SA, HC and LC between the two measurement points. In particular, SA in Grade 5 related to HC as well as LC in Grade 4. Further, SA in Grade 4 correlated moderately to HC in Grade 5. Besides several moderate relationships between student vocabulary knowledge and text comprehension, a rather high correlation was revealed for SA at the two measurement times ($r = .55$). A moderate correlation was also found for HC in Grades 4 and 5. Therefore, the results confirmed our expectation that the correlations between student semantic awareness and reading comprehension were stronger when compared to correlations between the aforementioned competences and grammar knowledge.

Profiles of language competence

To identify subgroups of students with different language competence profiles, the four subtests (LC, HC, SA, G) were included in the cluster analysis of the cases. The clustering was conducted separately for Grade 4 and Grade 5 results. The criteria for choosing the cluster solutions was: the theoretical meaning-fulness of a solution, acceptable homogeneity of clusters, and a sudden drop in the explained error sum of squares (EESS) for the solution (Bergman *et al.*, 2003). An 8-cluster solution was chosen for Grade 4 results (homogeneity less than 1.39, EESS = 68.26), and a 10-cluster solution for Grade 5 (homogeneity less than 1.99, EESS = 72.40). The principle for interpreting the clusters was as follows: if the standardized score of the variable fell between +.50 and –.50, the result was considered average. A result less than –.50 was considered low, and above .50 high. See Figure 1 for an illustration of the cluster profiles.

As expected, cluster profiles with all four language competences at the same level emerged (i.e., all high, average or low), but in addition, several profiles with more complex patterns were revealed.

Structural and individual stability of language competence profiles

To make meaningful inferences about the individual stability of the language competence profiles, we went on to study the structural compatibility of cluster pairs in Grades 4 and 5. The comparison of cluster centroids in Grade 4 and Grade 5 showed good compatibility, ASEDs were smaller than 1 for 7 cluster pairs out of 8, indicating good compatibility (Bergman *et al.*, 2003). The ASED between Cl4–8 and Cl5–8 was higher than acceptable; Cl5–9 and Cl5–10 were paired with dummies. See Figure 1 for details; comparable clusters have the same name ends (e.g. Cl4–1 and Cl5–1).

Next, the exact cell-wise analyses of a contingency table (EXACON) using an χ^2 test were conducted to reveal different significant developmental trajec-tories from Grade 4 to Grade 5. Several stable profiles emerged (see Figure 1, intact lines): stable mostly high (Cl4–1 to Cl5–1), stable high with low G (Cl4–2

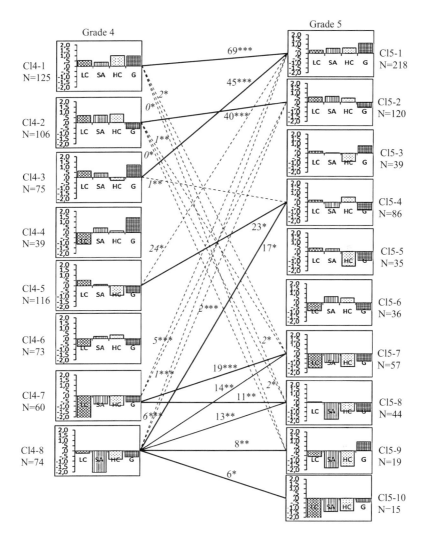

Figure 1: The structural compatibility and individual stability of language competence profiles from Grade 4 to Grade 5

Note: Z scores of subscales are presented. LC–*lower level text comprehension*, SA–*semantic awareness*, HC–*higher-level text comprehension*, G–*grammar knowledge*. Lines indicate *types* and dashed lines *antitypes*, numbers on lines show the number of students in *type/antitype*. *p < .05, **p < .005, ***p < .0005.

to Cl5–2), all low or mostly low (Cl4–7 to Cl5–7 or Cl5–8, Cl4–8 to Cl5–7 or Cl5–8 or Cl5–10). In addition, some typical changes in language competence profiles emerged. A significant number of students with a high LC and G profile in Grade 4 (Cl4–3) took an average LC plus other high profile (Cl5–1) in Grade 5. Another significant group of students had better HC but lower SA scores (change from Cl4–5 profile to Cl5–4). Last but not least, significantly more students appeared to move from a low SA, HC, G profile (Cl4–8) to a low SA and G but high HC profile (Cl5–4), and from the same Cl4–8 profile to a high G plus other low profile (Cl5–9) than it could have been expected by chance.

The following 11 antitypes (i.e. profile changes less frequent than it could be expected by chance) emerged (see Figure 1, dashed lines): from Cl4–1 to Cl5–8 and Cl5–9, from Cl4–2 to Cl5–7, Cl5–8 and Cl5–9 indicating that students with all high or high SA, LC, HC performed low in all subscales or low in SA, LC, HC in the following year less often than it could have been expected by chance. In addition, antitypes Cl4–7 to Cl5–1 or to Cl5–2, and Cl4–8 to Cl5–1 or to Cl5–2 indicate the rare possibility of an opposite change – from low profiles to high ones. In addition, lowering SA and G scores (profiles from Cl4–3 to Cl5–4), or significant increases in HC and G (from Cl4–5 to Cl5–1) were unlikely.

Discussion

A proficiency in language competence is considered to be an important factor for cognitive development in students. We examined the development of reading comprehension at different cognitive levels, semantic awareness and grammar knowledge in mother tongue among 4th and 5th grade boys and girls. Using variable- and person-oriented approaches in data analysis, differences were revealed at the group level as well as between subgroups of individuals with different language competence profiles.

First, we assessed language competence in mother tongue in Grades 4 and 5. In accordance with student cognitive development (Cain & Oakhill, 2011; Saxton, 2010), the improvement in all language skills was expected. In fact, it was found that student language proficiency did increase over the year, but not in all domains. In particular, the students achieved higher results in both reading comprehension tasks and grammar knowledge, but not in semantic awareness. The latter result contradicts earlier studies, where the growth of word recognition was found over time (Cain & Oakhill, 2011; Eason *et al.*, 2012). On the one hand, our finding can be explained by the multiple-choice vocabulary task in Grade 5. In addition to the words from Grade 4, it comprised some new incorrect and rare items, which may have misled students and caused more incorrect answers (Rodriguez, 2005). Therefore, by adding further options, the probability of obtaining the right answer by chance decreases. Furthermore, according to the U-shaped pattern found in cognitive psychology, in the first phases of studies (Grade 4 in our study) students use words correctly. This period is followed by a second-phase (Grade 5) when rare words cause mistakes. In the third-phase, these errors start to decrease (Siegler, 2004). We only measured language competence twice, and this must be kept in mind when generalizing the findings from our study.

Second, we examined differences in student language competence on the basis of gender. In accordance with earlier studies (Logan & Johnston, 2010; Sinka, 2008), we found that girls achieved significantly higher results in all language tasks. However, while the boys managed to perform a word recognition task in Grade 5 at the same level as the year before, the girls' performance declined over the same period. This result may be explained by the girls having a higher sensitivity to the number of items to choose from in the list. More specifically, an increase in items in this task decreased their chances of choosing correct answers randomly (see Rodriguez, 2005).

In the next phase of the study, we analyzed correlations between student language skills in Grades 4 and 5. In line with earlier studies (Eason *et al.*, 2012; Connor & Al'Otaiba, 2008), we expected that students with better knowledge of grammar and better word recognition skills were able to comprehend texts better. We found significant but weak correlations between student reading comprehension and grammar knowledge. The correlations between reading comprehension and semantic awareness were stronger. Such results are partially coherent with previous studies, where reciprocal correlations were found between different language competences (Cain & Oakhill, 2011; Eason *et al.*, 2012). In order to comprehend a text, students have to grasp the vocabulary and meanings of words as well as grammar patterns. To support reading comprehension, students should be provided with vocabulary tasks adapted to their skill level (Connor & Al'Otaiba, 2008). Furthermore, meaningful links between new words and concepts, and the students' everyday lives have also been suggested (Siegler, 2005).

Next, we studied possible subgroups of students with different profiles of language competence and how they changed between Grade 4 and Grade 5. Four tasks (reading at different cognitive levels, semantic awareness, and grammar knowledge) distinguished several language competence profiles for both grades. The largest subgroup of students had high language competence profiles in both grades. The number of students in this cluster increased significantly in Grade 5 (from 18.7% to 32.6%). The second largest subgroup in Grade 5 presented stable low knowledge in grammar and high on the remaining skills (17.9% of students). A significant proportion of students fell in this cluster in Grade 4 as well (15.8%). In addition, two clusters with stable low results in all competences and mostly low competences were also revealed in both grades. However, the number of students in both clusters declined in Grade 5. Such results are in line with earlier studies, which indicate that student performance in similar types of tasks usually improves with time (Bast & Reitsma, 1998; Rodriguez, 2005).

Then, three clusters with average results in higher-level text comprehension and varying results on the remaining competences were revealed for Grade 4. Several mixed subgroups were revealed with low results in higher-level text comprehension (four clusters), or conversely, high results in higher-level text comprehension (three clusters) in Grade 5. Surprisingly, no subgroups with average results in higher-level text comprehension emerged in Grade 5. That is, student results in more complex reading tasks either improved or worsened in Grade 5. This refers to the skills needed to organize information and make correct sentences in accordance with the text. Earlier studies have indicated that a lack of psycholinguistic and metacognitive skills may increase problems in such tasks (Gleason & Rathner, 2009; Skehan, 2008; see also Lenneberg, 1967).

By exploring the typical changes in student language competence profiles, different combinations and levels of language competence emerged. It appeared that 6.7% of students in Grade 5 improved in most language skills, except the reading task, which required then to recognize true and false sentences. More importantly, the results for those students decreased from high to average in this task. This indicates a lack of ability to memories and locate information in the text (Siegler, 2005; Skehan, 2008).

There were also students (3.4%), who improved their performance in higher-level text comprehension, but performed worse in semantic awareness. As the multiple-choice list of words in the Grade 5 test comprised more items, student progress in semantic awareness might have been inhibited (Rodriguez, 2005). A second profile with improving results in higher-level reading comprehension also emerged. In particular, significantly more students than it could have been expected by chance (2.5%) changed from a mostly low profile in Grade 4 to low semantic awareness and grammar, but high results in higher-level reading comprehension in Grade 5. Such findings may be explained by the development of the students' ability to process and extrapolate information (Siegler, 2005). Other students in this profile group moved into the high profile group in grammar knowledge and the low profile group in the remaining competences. This refers to the development of focus and memorizing skills in these students in Grade 5 (see also Skehan, 2008).

In summary, on the basis of several of the atypical changes in the student language competence profiles, it may be concluded that extreme changes were unusual (such transitions were non-existent or very rare). Changes from low language competence profiles to the high profiles, or the contrary, were less frequent than could have been expected by chance. This is in line with earlier studies (Siegler, 2004; Uibu & Tropp, 2012).

Limitations and conclusions

Some limitations of the study should be considered. First, we only used four tasks to assess student language competence. A greater variety of tasks and texts may have increased the reliability of the results. Second, student reading comprehension at different cognitive levels was only examined using a narrative text (a fable), which might be quite unusual for some students. Third, one year is too short of a period to make long-term conclusions about the development of student language competence over time. To determine the potential U-shaped pattern found in cognitive development (Siegler, 2004), a longer period of research with several measurement points is recommended. Fourth, no additional information about internal or external factors (e.g. cognitive abilities, motivation) was applied in the study. Distinctions in language skills in relation to student cognitive skills should also be assessed.

Nevertheless, this is a study with a longitudinal design and a sizable sample, which allowed us to draw out some valuable conclusions about student language development in higher primary grades. (1) Reading comprehension is related more closely to word recognition than grammar knowledge. (2) Girls' exhibited higher competences in the Estonian language than boys, but problems emerged in the progress of word recognition in Grade 5. (3) To promote student language competence it is essential to use tasks that are suited to the students' cognitive level. (4) The assessment of student language competence was rather sensitive to context (see Gleason & Rathner, 2009). More items in the multiple-choice questions caused more mistakes in similar types of tasks. This should be considered when compiling language tests for practice and research. (5) The researchers should keep in mind that the development of language skills is not straightforward and similar for every student; therefore, individual-level profiles of development and possible reciprocal causation of language skills should also be studied. (6) The presence of a U-shaped developmental trajectory (Siegler, 2004) in language competence is for some students of theoretical and practical importance. Therefore, future research on this is expected.

Acknowledgements

This work was supported in part by the Estonian Ministry of Education and Research (Grant No. 3-2/TA5966) and in part by the ESF Program Eduko (project No 1.2.0302.09-004) and ESF project No. 1.2.0401.09-0070.

References

Bast, J., & Reitsma, P. (1998). Analysing the development of individual differences in terms of Matthew effects in reading: Results from a Dutch longitudinal study. *Developmental Psychology, 34*(6), 1373–1399.

Bergman, L.R., Magnusson, D., & El Khouri, B.M. (2003). *Studying Individual Development in an Interindividual Context*. London: Lawrence Erlbaum Associates.

Cain, K., & Oakhill, J. (2011). Matthew effects in young readers: Reading comprehension and reading experience aid vocabulary development. *Journal of Learning Disabilities, 44*(5), 431–443.

Chomsky, N. (1964). The development of grammar in child language: Formal discussion. *Monographs of the Society for Research in Child Development, 64*, 35–39.

Cohen, L., Manion, L., & Morrison, K. (2007). *Research Methods in Education* (6th ed.). London, New York: Routledge.

Connor, C.M., & Al'Otaiba, S. (2008). *Literacy* (pp. 235–247). USA: Elsevier Inc.

Eason, S.H., Goldberg, L.F., Young, K.M., Geist, M.C., & Cutting, M.C. (2012). Reader–Text Interactions: How Differential Text and Question Types Influence Cognitive Skills Needed for Reading Comprehension. *Journal of Educational Psychology, 104*(3), 515–528.

Echols, L.D., West, R.F., Stanovich, K.E., & Zehr, K.S. (1996). Using children's literacy activities to predict growth in verbal cognitive skills: A longitudinal investigation. *Journal of Educational Psychology, 88*(2), 296–304.

Foorman, B.R., Schatschneider, C., Eakin, M.N., Flecher, J.M., Moats, L.C., & Francis, D.J. (2006). The impact of instructional practices in Grades 1 and 2 on reading and spelling achievement in high poverty schools. *Contemporary Educational Psychology, 31*, 1–29.

Gee, J.P. (2012). *Social Linguistics and Literacies. Ideology in Discourses* (4th ed., pp. 1–242). London and New York: Routledge.

Gleason, J.B., & Ratner, N.B. (2009). *The Development of Language* (7th ed., pp. 1–512). Boston: Allyn & Bacon.

Krathwohl, D.R. (2002). A Revision of Bloom's Taxonomy: An Overview. *Theory into Practice*, 41(4), 212–218.

Krashen, S.D. (1982). *Principles and Practice in Second Language Acquisition*, (pp. 125–190). Oxford etc.: Pergamon Press.

Lenneberg, E.H. (1968). *Biological foundations of language*, (pp. 1–489). New York etc.: Wiley.

Logan, S., & Johnston, R. (2010). Investigating gender differences in reading. *Educational Review, 62*(2), 175–187.

Pečjak, S., Podlesek, A., & Pirc, T. (2011). Model of reading comprehension for 5th grade students. *Studia Psychologica, 53*(1), 53–67.

Põhikooli ja gümnaasiumi riiklik õppekava. (2007). [The National Curriculum of Basic and Upper Secondary School Education of Estonia; in Estonian]. Riigi Teataja I 2007, 40, 294. Retrieved from https://www.riigiteataja.ee/ert/act.jsp?id=802290

Põhikooli riiklik õppekava. (2011). [The National Curriculum of Basic Education of Estonia; in Estonian]. Riigi Teataja 06. jaanuari 2011 maärus nr 1.

Puksand, H. (2012). Reading habits of the Estonian adolescents – the basis for lifelong learning. In J. Mikk, P. Luik, M. Veisson (Eds.), *Lifelong Learning and Teacher Development* (pp. 146–161). Frankfurt am Main: Peter Lang Verlag.

Rodriguez, M.C. (2005). Three options are optimal for multiple-choice items: A meta-analysis of 80 years of research. *Educational Measurement: Issues and Practice, 24*, 3–13.

Saxton, M. (2010). *Child Language: Acquisition and Development*, (pp. 51–66). London etc: Sage Publication Ltd.

Siegler, R. (2004). U-Shaped Interest in U-Shaped Development and What It Means. *Journal of Cognition and Development, 5*(1), 1–10.

Siegler, R. (2005). Children's learning. *American Psychologist, 60*, 769–778.

Sinka, M. (2008). *6. klassi eesti keele 2008. aasta riikliku tasemetöö analüüs* [The Analysis of Year 2008 Grade 6 State Tests in Estonian Language, in Estonian]. Retrieved from http://www.ekk.edu.ee/vvfiles/0/6_%20klassi_eesti_%20keele_%20tasemet_366_366%2 02008%20anal_374_374sx.pdf

Skehan, P. (2008). *A Cognitive Approach to Language Learning*. Oxford: Oxford University Press.

Soodla, P. (2010). Teachers' judgement of students' reading difficulties and factors related to its accuracy. In A. Toomela (Ed.), *Systemic Person-Oriented Study of Child Development in Early Primary School* (pp. 47–71). Frankfurt am Main: Peter Lang Verlag.

Uibu, K., & Tropp, K. (2012). Bilingual and monolingual students' linguistic competences and their development at Estonian primary school. In A. Toomela, E. Kikas (Eds.), *Children studying in a wrong language: Russian-speaking children in Estonian school. Twenty years after the collapse of the Soviet Union* (pp. 17–42). Frankfurt am Main: Peter Lang Verlag.

Uusen, A., & Müürsepp, M. (2010). Orthographic skills and teaching orthography in light of the renewed Estonian language syllabus. *Problems of Education in the 21st Century, 21,* 170–184.

Vardja, M. (2006). *6. klassi eesti keele riiklik tasemetöö 2006* [The State Test of Year 2006 in Estonian Language of Grade 6, in Estonian]. Retrieved from http://www.ekk.edu.ee/vvfiles/0/tasemetood_6kl_analuusid_2006.pdf

Appendix 1:   Factor loadings for scales of language competence tests

Descriptions of items	Grade 4				Grade 5			
	HC	SA	LC	G	HC	SA	LC	G
Reading task I								
1 Comprehension reading (CR)	**.77**	.19	.08	.04	**.70**	.20	.13	.08
2 CR	**.70**	.17	.18	.09	**.74**	.18	.07	.08
3 CR	**.67**	.16	.09	.09	**.65**	.22	.24	−.00
4 CR	**.65**	.02	−.09	.04	**.62**	−.11	.11	.03
5 CR	**.56**	.18	.27	.15	**.65**	.25	.13	.20
Vocabulary task								
1 Adjective	.24	**.74**	.07	.06	.04	**.64**	.37	−.06
2 Adjective	.15	**.73**	.05	.04	.14	**.71**	−.01	.23
3 Adverb	.15	**.71**	.18	.00	.30	**.52**	.31	.01
4 Verb	.02	**.60**	.26	.17	.17	**.63**	.06	.14
Reading task II								
1 True/false sentence (TFS)	.15	.05	**.69**	.05	.24	.08	**.67**	.01
2 TFS	.10	.08	**.62**	−.03	.21	.07	**.60**	.09
3 TFS	.06	.03	**.60**	.04	.07	.32	**.50**	−.03
4 TFS	.05	.23	**.50**	−.16	.23	.01	**.51**	.14
5 TFS	−.02	.18	**.48**	.22	−.08	.13	**.68**	.07
Spelling task								
1 Adverb and verb	.06	.04	−.05	**.83**	.03	.01	.04	**.78**
2 Adjective and noun	.13	.04	.07	**.80**	.08	.07	.08	**.80**
3 Noun and noun	.27	.29	.09	**.43**	.14	.19	.10	**.64**
Cronbach's α for respective scale items	.73	.71	.55	.58	.76	.64	.63	.64
Mean	3.24	3.07	4.28	1.22	3.88	2.96	4.45	1.34
SD	1.64	1.26	1.04	1.12	1.48	1.16	.98	1.11

Notes: Description of items is presented by tasks and language categories since concrete descriptions had Estonian-specific domains. HC–higher-level text comprehension, SA–semantic awareness, LC–lower level text comprehension, G–grammar knowledge. **Bold**: items included in the respective scale.

The Role of Learning Strategies in PISA 2009 in Estonia: Metacognitive Skillfulness Giving Readers a Head Start

Ülle Säälik[a,1], Antero Malin[b], Kari Nissinen[b]

[a]University of Tartu, [b]University of Jyväskylä

Abstract

The role of learning strategies in predicting and explaining PISA reading test results in Estonia at both school and student level was analyzed alongside common background and learning environment factors using multilevel modeling. The most effective explanatory variables were metacognitive learning strategies: *summarizing* alone explained 33% of the variation between schools and 16% of the variation between students within schools, *understanding* and *remembering* alone explained 29% and 13% respectively. The effect of the aforementioned metacognitive skills, associated with 1 OECD standard deviation increase in the index value, enhanced performance by 33 and 28 score points respectively. On the contrary, *memorization strategies* caused a decrease in reading literacy performance by 6 points. About one third of the differences between schools in the PISA reading literacy results in Estonia could be explained by differences between schools in using metacognitive learning strategies. Assuming the educational goal is to offer everyone equal opportunity to cope and succeed, it is highly relevant to follow such instructional practice in schools raising student awareness and promoting their skills of learning strategies.

Key words: learning strategies, metacognitive skills, reading literacy, PISA survey, multilevel modeling

Introduction

The Role of Learning Strategies in PISA 2009 in Estonia

The essence of educational studies is to improve and enhance student academic achievement or ability to cope with life in the future. Large-scale educational surveys give us an opportunity and an obligation to monitor and evaluate the level of achievement along with factors that are likely to enhance or diminish success to find out what can be done by teachers in schools to help our children

---

1   Address for correspondence: yllesaalik@hotmail.com

to learn and cope better. Methods that worked before may not meet the needs of contemporary life.

The current paper will provide an overview of the impact of learning strategies on academic performance, and identify the effect of different student, school or learning-related explanatory variables at student and school level.

Relationship Between Academic Performance and Ways of Learning

Recent studies have shown that student academic success depends on what is going on in the classrooms and how the students learn. Successful students are said to be aware of their own learning, evaluate their learning needs to generate strategies to meet these needs, and to implement useful strategies (Hacker *et al.*, 2009). To evaluate learning progress and set targets for learning improvement, children must be consciously aware of strategies in the decision-making process. They must be able to select the best strategies for problem solving and reflect their thinking before, during and after learning (Jones, 2007; Fisher & Williams, 2002).

A large meta-analysis by Wang, Haertel and Walberg (1993–1994) on the relative influences on student learning found that classroom instruction and climate had an important impact on student learning. Independent student practice appeared to be one indicator of successful learning. On the student's side, the highest influence on learning was attributed to comprehension monitoring, planning learning actions and evaluating the usefulness of strategies – all referred to as metacognitive processes.

Another meta–analysis by Hattie (2009) assessed how six factors contributed to child achievement: the child, the home, the school, the curricula, the teacher and teaching approaches. The factor teaching approaches included study skills, which had a medium effect on child achievement (d=0.59), and metacognitive instruction in reading comprehension, which had a high effect (d=0.69).

Metacognition in Learning

The advanced thinking ability known as metacognition has been stated as the cognition of one's own cognitive processes (Flavell, 1976, 1979; Baker, 2002), at first mostly concerning memory. Soon the study of metacognition was found to relate to the field of reading comprehension (Brown, 1980; Brown *et al.*, 1983, Baker & Brown 1984). Metacognition as such has been defined in terms of several aspects: awareness of people experiencing cognitions, awareness of one's own cognitive processes as they relate to the task, monitoring of cognitive processes for their efficiency, and the ability to regulate cognition to improve effectiveness or using strategies to repair comprehension failures (William & Atkins, 2009).

Metacognitive learning skills have been found to have a highly positive effect on improving learning results, they appear to be strong predictors of academic performance, and they are possible to develop with training independent of the student's intellectual ability (Pennequin *et al.*, 2010; van der Stel & Veenman, 2010). The teacher's role in developing metacognitive awareness in children, through discussion while learning (self–reflection, planning the work, evaluating etc.) can be crucial; therefore, it is in the teacher's hands to promote effective learning skills by encouraging pupils to articulate their thoughts about their learning (Jones, 2007).

Since metacognition has such an essential role in improving learning results, and as it is largely the teachers that can and should teach learning skills, questions could be posed as to whether such skills are being systematically developed in schools or not. Representative research data are needed as a plausible basis for drawing some general conclusions.

Assessing Learning Strategies in PISA Studies

PISA, the Programme for International Student Assessment undertaken by the Organisation for Economic Cooperation and Development (OECD), is a large-scale on-going programme for monitoring performance in reading, math and science among 15-year-olds. In 2009, when reading literacy was the main assessment component, 67 countries participated in the study (OECD, 2010a). It was the second time that Estonia had participated in such a comprehensive educational study. A large-scale student assessment with representative national samples, such as PISA, offers a wide variety of data for exploring the current situation in schools. By analyzing the relationship between student test scores and their responses about their learning skills, it should be possible to detect trends in educational practices in schools.

Student use of learning strategies such as memorization, elaboration and control strategies have been explored in PISA studies for years. The 2009 PISA study included questions on student awareness and the likely use of different reading or learning strategies, including metacognitive awareness and the use of summarizing skills (OECD, 2010a; OECD, 2010b). New data about student learning skills make it possible to analyze the effect of those skills on academic results, and to distinguish those most useful in this respect. A previous analysis of PISA 2009 Estonian data showed that low-performing students tend to report less use of metacognitive skills and more traditional methods such as memorizing or control strategies (Mikk *et al.*, 2012). Thus, the relationship between high performance in PISA and metacognitive awareness was discovered, but whether the effect of metacognitive skills could be attributed to students or is dependent on the school should be revealed to draw conclusions on possible differences in teaching practice in schools.

In most PISA countries, a great share of the variation in student performance has been attributable to differences between schools (Malin, 2005; OECD, 2010c), so this might be the case in Estonia as well. When a study discovers evidence of between-school variability explained by metacognitive skills and awareness, we can assume that the development of these skills is greater in some schools than in other schools.

When discovering a systematic variation in academic performance, it might be possible to trace the factors describing the "source" of this variation while also exposing subgroups performing at the lower level (Malin, 2005, 22). Children who are struggling readers also typically have certain background characteristics such as male gender, low socio–economic status plus some factors from the classroom environment, such as a disruptive disciplinary climate or poor teacher-student relationship (Garbe *et al*, 2010; OECD, 2010b).

Influencing Background Factors

When analyzing influence on learning outcomes, several common background factors that disadvantage student progress at both individual and school level have been pointed out when describing different kinds of academic results. The socio-economic background of students and schools is said to appear to have a powerful influence on performance, although low socio-economic status does not necessarily result in poor performance (OECD, 2010a).

Gender differences in academic performance are constantly a point of focus in educational research. Reading literacy assessments such as PIRLS or PISA have confirmed a gender gap existing in favor of girls, and comparing PISA studies between 2000–2009 the gender gap has even increased (Mullis *et al,*

2012; OECD, 2010b). In the 2009 PISA study in OECD countries, the difference between mean reading scores for boys and girls was 39 points, in Estonia the gap was as high as 44 points (Tire *et al*, 2010). The OECD analyses imply that approaches to learning actually mediate the gender gap in reading performance, so that if the boys had the same level of awareness of metacognitive skills, their results could be around 15 points higher (OECD, 2010b).

Although PISA tests and questionnaires are translated into all the main languages spoken in a country, the schools or regions of minority languages often show lower results. In Estonia the pupils in Russian-speaking schools have performed at a lower reading level than their peers in Estonian-speaking schools (Tire *et al.*, 2010). Similar effects, where students speaking the minority language tend to perform lower, in spite of being educated with their own language, have also been observed in other countries; for example, in Finland where the Swedish language is the minority language the students in Swedish-speaking schools have shown lower results (Harju–Luukkainen & Nissinen, 2011).

When revealing the effect of learning-associated variables on student learning outcomes it is essential to consider relevant background factors in order to evaluate their relative importance. Background factors are rather permanent, and teaching hardly affects them, but it should be possible to modify the learning environment and learning skills with appropriate instructional practice. Our interest in this study was to find out what appears to matter more, how much emphasis can be put on learning skills compared to other factors.

Research Questions

The aim of the paper is to study the role of different learning strategies in explaining PISA reading test results in Estonia at school and student level, alongside common background and learning environment factors. The research problems were set as follows:
• What is the effect of learning strategies, background factors and learning environment factors on PISA reading scores?
• How much of the between-school and student variation in reading literacy performance is attributable to learning strategies, background factors and learning environment factors?

Data and Methods

Sample

In the PISA 2009 study in Estonia, a two-stage stratified sample design was used. At the first stage, individual schools with 15-year-old students were sampled systematically from a comprehensive national list of schools with probabilities that were proportional to a measure of size – the number of PISA-eligible 15-year-old students enrolled in the school. At the second stage, the students were randomly sampled within each sampled school. A sample typically of 35 students was selected; and if there were fewer than 35 eligible students in the school, all students on the list were selected (OECD, 2012). Altogether, 4,727 students from 175 schools participated (51% boys, 49% girls), forming a representative sample of 15-year-old students in Estonia. There were 3,734 (79%) students from 138 Estonian-speaking schools, 867 (18.3%) from 31 Russian-speaking schools and 126 (2.7%) from 6 schools with mixed language. In statistical analyses, the Russian-speaking and mixed language schools were combined in one group, due to the small number of mixed language schools and students.

Data Collection

As a part of the PISA study, each student filled in a pencil-and-paper reading literacy test booklet with either multiple-choice, closed-constructed response items or open answers requiring students to develop their own responses designed to measure broader constructs. After the test, students answered a questionnaire about their personal background, their learning habits, their attitudes towards reading, and their engagement and motivation (OECD, 2010a).

Test Scores and Indices in PISA Data

The test scores from the PISA data have been derived from student responses using item-response methodology, specifically the Rasch model (OECD, 2009). In determining the scores, PISA uses the methodology usually known as plausible values (Wu, 2005), which is reported to possess favorable properties in regard to estimating population-level statistics (OECD 2009). A plausible value is an estimate of the latent proficiency of a student who has attained a certain raw score in the test. The plausible values calculated for students take the role of 'test score' used as response variables in statistical analyses. In PISA data sets, the plausible values are scaled to have the international (OECD) average of 500 and standard deviation of 100. To overcome the uncertainty in estimating unobserved proficiencies, PISA has adopted an approach where five different plausible values are calculated for each student. Each student has five different equally likely proficiency estimates (OECD, 2010a; OECD, 2012).

The adequate procedure for statistical analyses using plausible values is to perform similar analyses with each plausible value and then apply a multiple imputation methodology to incorporate the five different results into one final result (OECD, 2009). This way the extra variation due to imputation is properly taken into account. However, it can be very demanding to apply the complete multiple imputation approach with all plausible values to more advanced statistical analyses (e.g. multilevel modeling). Since the plausible values of a student are highly correlated, an approximate analysis can be obtained in a less complicated way by selecting just one plausible value and performing the analysis with it. This simpler approach was adopted here.

The indices were constructed through the scaling of items from student questionnaires, and then standardized so that the mean of the index value for the OECD student population was 0 and the standard deviation was 1, countries being given equal weight in the standardization process (OECD, 2012, 280). A more complete overview of indices used in the analysis is given in Appendix 1.

Statistical Analyses

As the data are hierarchically structured on two levels, and the students are nested within schools, the statistical analyses were conducted using multilevel models (Goldstein, 2011). Multilevel modeling makes it possible to draw correct statistical inference for regression-type analyses under the hierarchical data structure.

Only one explanatory variable was used at a time in the multilevel models to identify the individual effect of each variable on reading literacy score. The variance components of each model were compared to the null model, which was the simple variance component model without any explanatory variable. This model only divides the total variance into two variance components, describing the variation between schools and between students within schools. The proportional reduction in variance components (Snijders & Bosker, 2002) was used as a measure for the explained proportion of variance.

The statistical analyses were conducted using MLwiN software (Rasbash *et al.*, 2012). Student weights were used in modeling.

Results

Descriptive Statistical Results

With descriptive statistics it is possible to see the basis for this analysis, the differences in reading literacy scores and levels of indices. Table 1 shows the mean value of reading literacy scores (based on plausible value 1, with standard deviations in parentheses). This is higher in Estonian-speaking schools than in Russian and Mixed language schools. The boys tend to perform at a lower level in both types of schools compared to girls: in Estonian-speaking schools the mean for girls is 532 (SD=72) and for boys 489 (SD=78) score points; in Russian or Mixed language schools these figures are 499 (SD=74) and 459 (SD=76) respectively.

Table 1: *Mean reading literacy score and standard deviation on the basis of gender and school language*

School language	Gender	N	Mean	SD
Estonian	Female	1812	532	72
	Male	1922	489	78
	Total	3734	510	78
Russian + mixed	Female	485	499	74
	Male	508	459	76
	Total	993	479	77

The comparison of indices of learning strategies in Table 2 shows us that the awareness and use of metacognitive skills, such as understanding and remembering (UNDREM) or summarizing (METASUM) in Estonia is highest among girls in Estonian-speaking schools, and higher than the average in OECD countries. The boys in Estonian-speaking schools and the girls in Russian or Mixed language schools reported the use of metacognitive skills closer to the average in OECD countries. The lowest average use of metacognitive skills in Estonia was reported by boys in Russian or Mixed language schools.

The students in Russian or Mixed language schools reported the active use of memorization (MEMOR) with indices of 0.49 for girls and 0.29 for boys, whereas the mean index for students in Estonian-speaking schools was close to the OECD average (0.09 and –0.08, respectively). The control strategies (CSTRAT) were not so often used by boys irrespective of school language;

elaboration strategies (ELAB) were used by all student groups in Estonia near the OECD average level.

Table 2:   *Mean index and standard deviation of learning strategies, teacher-student relations, disciplinary climate and socio-economic status on the basis of gender and school language*

School language	Gender		UND–REM	META–SUM	ME-MOR	ELAB	C–STRAT	STUD–REL	DIS–CLIMA	ESCS
Estonian	Female	Mean	0.51	0.42	0.09	0.05	0.01	0.05	–0.02	0.18
		SD	0.85	0.79	0.81	0.85	0.81	0.85	0.97	0.8
	Male	Mean	0.11	0.01	–0.08	0.11	–0.23	–0.13	–0.05	0.23
		SD	0.99	0.93	0.81	0.84	0.83	0.86	0.9	0.81
Russian + mixed	Female	Mean	0.13	0.18	0.49	0.08	–0.07	0.02	0.36	0.04
		SD	0.90	0.84	0.84	0.86	0.78	0.79	0.97	0.68
	Male	Mean	–0.06	–0.2	0.29	0.2	–0.26	–0.06	0.39	0.08
		SD	0.96	0.93	0.81	0.88	0.82	0.81	0.98	0.73

Note. Indices were scaled so that OECD mean=0 and SD=1. A complete explanation of variables is given in Appendix 1.

The indicators from the classroom and learning environment show significant differences between Estonian and Russian-Mixed language schools. The index of disciplinary climate (DISCLIMA) in Estonian-speaking schools is close to the OECD average, but in Russian or Mixed language schools the students tended to report this more positively. Teacher-student relations (STUDREL) on the basis of gender were assessed as being similar in both types of schools. Socio-economic status was assessed as being near the OECD average among Russian or Mixed language school students and slightly higher than the OECD average among Estonian-speaking school students.

Effects on Reading Literacy Performance

The regression coefficient estimates from the one-factor multilevel models in Table 3 reveal the effect of each variable alone on reading literacy test scores. Since the indices were scaled so that the OECD standard deviation is 1, the regression coefficient estimates are equal to the effect of 1 OECD standard deviation increase in the index value. The Estonian standard deviations are slightly smaller than those for the OECD (cf. Table 2).

On average, the reading literacy score for the girls was 40 points higher than for the boys. Students in Russian or Mixed language schools had an average score that was 31 points lower. The rise in the level of economic, social and cultural status (ESCS, definition according to PISA study explained in Appendix 1) by 1 unit was associated with a rise of 19 points in the reading literacy score. The metacognitive skills such as summarizing (METASUM) and understanding-remembering (UNDREM), when increased by 1 index unit, would help enhance reading literacy performance by 33 and 28 points respectively. By contrast, memorizing (MEMOR), when applied by students with a 1 unit higher index value, caused a decrease in reading literacy performance of 6 points. Other learning strategies such as control strategies (CSTRAT) or elaboration (ELAB) could give a relatively small increase by 12 and 7 points respectively. Variables describing the learning environment, such as teacher-student relations (STUDREL) and disciplinary climate (DISCLIMA), with their coefficients of 17 and 11, also showed a positive effect on improving reading literacy performance when increased by 1 unit, but clearly less than the metacognitive skills.

Table 3: *Regression coefficient estimates from one-factor multilevel models with standard errors and p-values*

Model No	Variable	Coeff.	S.E.	p
1	Gender (female)	40.2	2.07	<.001
2	School language (russmix)	−31.2	7.20	<.001
3	ESCS	19.1	1.44	<.001
4	METASUM	33.3	1.14	<.001
5	UNDREM	27.6	1.10	<.001
6	MEMOR	−5.9	1.56	<.001
7	ELAB	7.2	1.46	<.001
8	CSTRAT	12.4	1.42	<.001
9	DISCLIMA	10.6	1.61	<.001
10	STUDREL	17.0	1.46	<.001

Explaining Variance at the School and Student Level

Table 4 presents how much of the variation in reading literacy score each factor alone explains between schools and between students within schools, as well as of the total variance. The simple variance component model has been applied here without any explanatory variable. This model only divides the total variance between two components, describing the variation between schools and between students within schools. In reading literacy score, the variance components are 1,408 and 5,364, and the total variance is 6,772. From these numbers we can calculate, by dividing the between-school variance component by the total variance, that intra-class correlation (ICC) in reading literacy was 0.21. This means that 21% of the total variance in reading literacy scores was due to differences between schools in their average performance in the PISA reading literacy test.

The analysis reveals that schools in Estonia differ in regard to useful ways to learn. Learning strategies, especially metacognitive strategies, have significant effects on reading literacy performance at student level, but even more at school level. Of the metacognitive strategies, summarizing alone explained 33% of the variation between schools and 16% of the variation between students within schools. Understanding and remembering explained 29% and 13%, respectively. Other learning strategies tended to be relatively weak in explaining the test scores (memorizing about 2% at school level and 0.4% at student level, control strategies 9% and 2%, and elaboration strategies 3% and 1% respectively).

Table 4: *How much each factor alone explains the variation between and within schools (%)*

Model No		Explanatory variable	Between schools	Within schools	Total variance
1	Back-ground	ESCS	24.6	3.3	7.7
2		Gender	4.4	7.5	6.8
3		School language	11.5	0.0	2.4
4	Learning strategies	Metacognition: summarizing	32.7	16.4	19.8
5		Metacognition: understanding and remembering	29.3	13.1	16.5
6		Memorizing	1.5	0.4	0.7
7		Control strategies	8.7	2.0	3.4
8		Elaboration strategies	3.1	1.0	1.4
9	Learning environment	Teacher–student relations	5.0	3.7	4.0
10		Disciplinary climate	3.1	1.6	1.9

The student's economic, social and cultural status (ESCS) seemed to have the highest explanatory power among background variables at the school level. ESCS alone explained 25% of the between-school variation, but only 3% of the variation between students within schools. Gender alone explained more at the individual level than the school level, but both with a relatively minor effect at about 8% and 4% respectively. School language alone explained about 12% of between-school variation. It could not explain the variation between students within schools since the only schools with both Estonian and Russian language were grouped with the Russian schools.

Variables describing the classroom learning environment (teacher-student relations and disciplinary climate) tended to be relatively weak in explaining reading literacy performance when taken alone in the model, around 2–5% of the variance at different levels.

The most effective explanatory variables were the metacognitive learning strategies: summarizing and understanding-remembering. Together they explained 43% of the variation in reading literacy score between schools, 21% of the variation between students within schools and 26% of the total variance. Together with ESCS, they explained no less than 56% of the variation between schools, 23% of the variation–between students within schools and 30% of the total variance.

Discussion

Several educational studies have proven that how students learn is closely related to their learning outcomes; for example, the meta-analyses by Hattie (2009) or Wang *et al.* (1993–1994). The present research confirms this, finding that learning strategies can be even stronger predictors in explaining reading literacy test results in the PISA 2009 study in Estonia than commonly known important background factors. The metacognitive learning strategies were found to have a relatively strong effect, and they explained a large part of the variance both at student and school levels.

During the last few decades, metacognitive skillfulness has been a point of focus for educational studies; and its crucial role in improving learning outcomes was supported in the present study, just as many before have stressed (Flavell, 1976, 1979; Baker, 2002; Brown, 1980; Brown *et al.*, 2009; Pennequin *et al.*, 2010; van der Stel & Veenman, 2010). In the case of real-life reading tasks similar to the tasks in the PISA reading literacy test, metacognitive learning skills help much more than traditional ways of learning such as elaboration or control strategies. Learning by heart (memorizing), on the contrary, might even cause failure.

Teachers are able to contribute to their students' success in many ways. Promoting a positive learning atmosphere and relations with students seems obvious, but in the present study they appeared to be of secondary importance. Nevertheless, that does not diminish the teacher's role in student success altogether, as developing learning skills is still in the teachers' hands: helping students through dialogic teaching using open questions, guiding them towards developing skills through self-reflective discussion, instructing others and so on (Jones, 2007; Pennequin *et al.*, 2010; van der Stel & Veenman, 2010). Less successful teachers may rely more on traditional closed forms of questioning, but these 'right answer' methods do not help develop high-level reading skills (Mercer & Howe, 2012).

A prior study of PISA 2009 Estonian data revealed positive correlations between academic results and the level of metacognitive skillfulness, as mentioned in Mikk *et al.* (2012), yet the source of such correlations was not revealed. The current study sheds more light on the essence of this topic, indicating that metacognitive skillfulness really has a high impact on results, but its level is significantly dependent on the school. It was also discovered that student ability to choose effective learning strategies is more important than background factors or classroom climate factors.

Since the development of metacognitive skills demands more talking rather than quiet in the classroom, this helps us understand why the disciplinary climate was reported as high in Russian-speaking schools, but metacognitive skillfulness was low. If the teaching tradition sees quiet in the classroom as an indicator of 'good' teaching, then metacognitive learning skills are unlikely to be promoted. However, for further developments, the role of language could be investigated more precisely to see whether or how much the language gap depends on metacognition, other learning strategies, and learning environmental factors.

The analysis revealed that schools in Estonia do differ in terms of the level of useful ways of learning. Each metacognitive learning strategy alone explained about one third of the differences between schools in PISA reading literacy results in Estonia. This finding confirms the proposed assumption that differences in student results might be affected by differences between schools in Estonia; some schools probably encourage metacognitive skillfulness, while others not that much. If the educational goal is to offer everyone equal opportunity to cope and succeed, it is highly relevant to follow such instructional practices in schools that raise student awareness and promote skillful use of learning strategies.

Directions for Future Research

Since the present analysis was conducted on the data of a single country, a comparative study including more countries is needed in future research to reveal possible patterns or sources of the effects of learning strategies. The roles of background factors affecting skillfulness in learning strategies should also be studied in a more detailed way to distinguish the combinations of elements of effect or more precise sources of effect.

Acknowledgement

This research was supported by the European Social Fund Doctoral Studies and Internationalization Programme DoRa administered by the Archimedes Foundation, and initial support from the European Social Fund EDUKO programme, grant No. 1.2.0302.09–004.

References

Baker, L., & Brown, A.L. (1984). Metacognitive skills and reading. In P. D. Pearson, R. Barr, M. L. Kamil, & P. Mosenthal (Eds.), *Handbook of Reading Research* (pp. 353–394), NY: Longman.

Baker, L. (2002). Metacognition in comprehension instruction. In C. Block, & M. Pressley (Eds.), *Comprehension instruction: Research–based best practices* (pp.77–95). NY: Guilford.

Brown, A. L. (1980). Metacognitive development and reading. In R. J. Spiro, B. Bruce, & W. Brewer (Eds.), *Theoretical issues in reading comprehension* (pp. 453–482). Hillsdale, NJ: Lawrence Erlbaum Associates.

Brown, A. L., Bransford, J. D., Ferrara, R. A., & Campione, J.C. (1983). Learning, re-membering, and understanding. In J. H. Flavell, & E. M. Markman (Eds.), *Handbook of child psychology,* III (pp. 77–166), New York: Wiley.

Fisher, R., & Williams, M. (2002). *Unlocking writing,* London: David Fulton.

Flavell, J. H. (1976). Metacognitive aspects of problem solving. In L. B. Resnick (Ed.), *The nature of intelligence* (pp. 231–235). Hillsdale, NJ: Lawrence Erlbaum Associates.

Flavell, J. H. (1979). Metacognition and cognitive monitoring: A new area of cognitive–developmental inquiry. *American Psychologist, 34,* 906–911.

Garbe, C., Holle, K., Weinhold, S., Meyer–Hamme A., & Barton, A. (2010). Characteristics of adolescent struggling readers. In C. Garbe, K. Holle, S. Weinhold (Eds.) *ADORE– Teaching struggling adolescent readers in European countries. Key elements of good practice* (pp. 1–44). Frankfurt am Main: Peter Lang.

Goldstein, H. (2011). *Multilevel statistical models*, 4th edition. Chichester: Wiley.

Hacker, D. J., Dunlosky, J., & Graesser, A.C. (2009). A growing sense of "agency". In J. D. Hacker, J. Dunlosky, & A. C. Graesser (Eds) *Handbook of Metacognition in Education* (pp. 1–4), NY: Routledge.

Harju–Luukkainen, H., & Nissinen, K. (2011). *Finlandssvenska 15–åriga elevers resultatnivå I PISA 2009 –undersökningen.* Jyväskylä: Finnish Institute for Educational research. (note: in Swedish)

Hattie, J. A. C. (2009). *Visible learning: A synthesis of meta-analyses relating to achievement.* New York: Routledge

Jones, D. (2007). Speaking, listening, planning and assessing: the teacher's role in developing metacognitive awareness / *Early Child Development and Care*, 177(6 & 7), 569–579. doi: 10.1080/03004430701378977

OECD (2009). *PISA Data Analysis Manual: SAS, Second Edition.* OECD Publishing.

OECD (2010a). *PISA 2009 Assessment Framework: Key Competencies in Reading, Mathematics and Science*, Retrieved from http://www.oecd.org/dataoecd/11/40/44455820.pdf

OECD (2010b). *PISA 2009 results: Learning to learn– student engagement, strategies and practices (Vol III)*, http://dx.doi.org/10.178/9789264083943–en

OECD (2010c). *PISA 2009 Results: What Makes a School Successful? – Resources, Policies and Practices (Vol IV)*, http://dx.doi.org/10.1787/9789264091559–en

OECD (2012). *PISA 2009 Technical Report*, http://dx.doi.org/10.1787/9789264167872–en

Malin, A. (2005) *School differences and inequities in educational outcomes. PISA 2000 results of reading literacy in Finland.* (Doctoral dissertation). University of Jyväskylä.

Mercer, N., & Howe, C. (2012). Explaining the dialogic processes of teaching and learning: The value and potential of sociocultural theory. *Learning, Culture and Social Interaction 1*, 12–21.

Mikk, J., Kitsing, M., Must, O., Säälik, Ü., & Täht, K. (2012) *Eesti PISA 2009 kontekstis: tugevused ja probleemid. Programmi Eduko uuringutoetuse kasutamise lepingu aruanne* [Estonia in PISA 2009 context: strengths and issues. The Eduko programme grant report].Retrieved from Estonian Ministry of Education and Research website: http://www.hm.ee/index.php?048181

Mullis, I. V. S., Martin, M. O., Foy, P., & Drucker, K. T. (2012). *The PIRLS 2011 International Results in Reading.* Chestnut Hill, MA: TIMSS & PIRLS International Study Center, Retrieved from http://timss.bc.edu/pirls2011/downloads/P11_IR_FullBook.pdf

Pennequin, V., Sorel, O., Nanty, I., & Fontaine, R. (2010). Metacognition and low achievement in mathematics: The effect of training in the use of metacognitive skills to solve mathematical word problems. *Thinking & Reasoning*, 16(3), 198–220

Rasbash, J., Steele, F., Browne, W. J., & Goldstein, H. (2012). *A User's Guide to MLwiN. Version 2.26*. Centre for Multilevel Modelling, University of Bristol.

Snijders, T. & Bosker, R. (2002). *Multilevel Analysis. An Introduction to Basic and Advanced Multilevel Modeling*. London: Sage Publications.

Tire, G., Puksand, H., Henno, I., & Lepmann, T. (2010). *PISA 2009–Eesti tulemused. Eesti 15–aastaste õpilaste teadmised ja oskused funktsionaalses lugemises, matemaatikas ja loodusteadustes*. Retrieved from http://www.ekk.edu.ee/vvfiles/0/PISA_2009_Eesti.pdf

van der Stel, M., & Veenman M. V. J. (2010). Development of metacognitive skillfulness: A Longitudinal study. *Learning and Individual Differences* 20, 220–224, Elsevier. doi: 10.1016/j.lindif.2009.11.005

Wang, M. C., Haertel, G. D., & Walberg, H. J. (1994) What helps students learn?, *Educational Leadership*, December 1993–January 1994, pp. 74–79

Williams, J. P., & Atkins, J. G. (2009) The role of metacognition in teaching reading comprehension to primary students. In J. D. Hacker, J. Dunlosky, & A. C. Graesser (Eds) *Handbook of Metacognition in Education* (pp. 26–43), New York: Routledge.

Wu, M. (2005). The role of plausible values in large-scale surveys. Studies in Educational Evaluation, 31, 114–128.

Appendix 1: *Description of student background questionnaire indices for the PISA study used in the paper*

Name of the index	Acronym	Sample questions
Metacognition: Understanding and remembering	UNDREM	Reading task: You have to understand and remember the information in a text. *How do you rate the usefulness of the following strategies for understanding and memorizing the text? (Answers on a six-point scale)* A) I concentrate on the parts of the text that are easy to understand; B) I quickly read through the text twice; C) After reading the text, I discuss its content with other people; D) I underline important parts of the text; E) I summarize the text in my own words; and F) I read the text aloud to another person.
Metacognition: Summarizing	METASUM	You have just read a long and rather difficult two-page text about fluctuations in the water level of a lake in Africa. You have to write a summary. How do you rate the usefulness of the following strategies for writing a summary of this two-page text? *(Answers on a six-point scale)* A) I write a summary. Then I check that each paragraph is covered in the summary, because the content of each paragraph should be included; B) I try to copy out accurately as many sentences as possible; C) before writing the summary, I read the text as many times as possible; D) I carefully check whether the most important facts in the text are represented in the summary; and E) I read through the text, underlining the most important sentences, then I write them in my own words as a summary.
Control strategies	CSTRAT	When you are studying, how often do you do the following? *(Answers on a four-point scale)* When I study, I start by figuring out what exactly I need to learn When I study, I check if I understand what I have read When I study, I make sure that I remember the most important points in the text
Memorization strategies	MEMOR	When you are studying, how often do you do the following? *(Answers on a four-point scale)* When I study, I try to memorize as many details as possible When I study, I read the text over and over again

Appendix 1:   *Continuation*

Name of the index	Acronym	Sample questions
Elaboration strategies	ELAB	When you are studying, how often do you do the following? *(Answers on a four-point scale)* When I study, I try to relate new information to prior knowledge acquired in other subjects When I study, I figure out how the information might be useful outside school
Economic, social and cultural status	ESCS	The index is calculated relying on the highest occupational status of the parents (HISEI), highest educational level of the parents in years of education according to ISCED (PARED), and home possessions (HOMEPOS)
Teacher-student relations	STUDREL	To what extent do you agree or disagree with the following statements? *(Answers on a four-point scale)* I get along well with most of my teachers Most of my teachers are interested in my well-being Most of my teachers really listen to what I have to say If I need extra help, I will receive it from my teachers Most of my teachers treat me fairly
Disciplinary climate	DISCLIMA	How often do these things happen in your test language lessons? *(Answers on a four-point scale)* Students don't listen to what the teacher says There is noise and disorder Students don't start working for a long time after the lesson begins

Differences in the Argumentation of State Examination Compositions by Male and Female Students of Various School Types

Merle Kaldjärv[1]
Tallinn University

Abstract

In order to determine argumentative skills, the preferences in the argumentation structure adopted by students of different school types have been established. This constitutes a current topic as there were significant changes in the form of the state Estonian language examination in 2012 and the argumentative text type will be given higher priority than in the previous format. The aim of the present article is to analyze whether there are differences in the argumentation in state exam compositions written by male and female students of various school types. The application of the argumentation structure will be analyzed on the basis of the argumentation across the whole text of the state exam composition. With reference to the third paragraph of the composition, five most widely used discussion types are formulated. On the basis of the study it may be concluded that there were essential differences in the argumentative skills of male and female students of different school types.

Key words: argumentation structure, test of significance, the Estonian language

Introduction

In order to graduate from secondary school, students must complete the state exam composition, a national Estonian language examination. The exam is compulsory for secondary school graduates; only students studying Estonian as a second language may take the Estonian language as the second language examination instead. The exam consists of an argumentative composition in which the writer presents arguments and counterarguments with respective substantiations and conclusions.

When the state examinations were introduced in 1997, serious discussions about students' poor reasoning skills arose immediately. Changes related to the alterations to state examination compositions in 2012 have once again given rise to fundamental discussions. There will be significant changes in the format of

---

1   Address for correspondence: kaldjarv@tlu.ee

the Estonian language state examination: the minimum 400-word composition must focus on a problem based on a given text. The new format requires even better skills in reasoning, analysis and synthesis.

This article presents part of a broader study, "Argumentation in State Examination Compositions", which provides an overview of students' argumentative skills in 1997, 2004–2006 and 2008. In order to improve skills in composing texts based on argumentation, it is important to study the choices made in the argumentation of earlier state exam compositions (texts of at least 600 words). Although argumentation in state exam compositions has been analyzed previously (Lepajõe, 2002; Hennoste, 2005), none of the studies so far have been based on such a wide sample nor used the content analysis method, enabling the simultaneous use of both quantitative and qualitative approaches.

The aim of the present article is to determine the statistically significant differences in composition argumentation by gender and various school types. One of the reasons given for changing the state examination is poor exam results. The grades awarded to compositions written by men are lower than those by women. The state exam update aims to find a solution to the problem of how to raise the exam grades. According to the state examination evaluation criteria, the writer of the state examination composition is given the highest score for writing a text characteristic of the composition text type and for the use of argumentation.

The research question of the present article is to determine the differences in the argumentation of the state exam compositions between men and women by different school types.

In order to reach the aim, the following research tasks were set:
1) to reveal the structure of argumentation (SPEC) and macrostructures used in determining the argumentation in state exam compositions on the basis of one exam composition
2) to use the test of significance to determine the differences in the argumentation of the state exam compositions between men and women by different school types

The section following the introduction explains the study's theoretical basis. The section on the empirical data analysis focuses on argumentation at the paragraph and text level and on the possible differences in the argumentative skills between male and female students. This section also includes the comparative results of the argumentation used by the students from different school types in 2004–2006.

The Theoretical Basis of the Research

The article is based on the author's doctoral thesis studying argumentation in state examination compositions. The research aims to determine how students present their argumentation in composition texts. The study relies upon the internationally acknowledged principle of analyzing argumentation on the basis of rhetoric, logic and dialectics (Rehg, 2001). The appropriate theoretical basis to connect the given areas is pragmatics (Mey, 2001; Õim, 1986) taking the language use analysis onto a more abstract textual level.

In describing and interpreting the data in the doctoral thesis, the author relied on macrostructures (Dijk, 1980), the structure of argumentation (Kaldjärv, 2007), speech acts (Austin, 1962; Searle, 1969), communication principles (Grice, 1975, 1989), linguistic pragmatics (Levinson, 1983; Mey, 2001; Õim, 1986), problem solving (Hoey, 1979; 1994; 2001) and the pragma-dialectical argumentation theory (Eemeren, Grootendorst, 1992, 2004). The research employed directed content analysis (Krippendorff, 1980) enabling the numerical determination of the elements of argumentation structure in the text.

Argumentation, i.e., substantiation, is based on logic; in the given discipline an argument is considered as the basis of the reason or proof which is part of the proof structure (Grauberg, 1996, pp. 79). The logical structure of demonstration includes: 1) a thesis, i.e., a statement whose validity is to be substantiated; 2) reasons, i.e., arguments by which the validity is demonstrated; 3) demonstration connecting the reasons with the thesis (Vuks, 1999, pp. 181). Argumentation is a broader concept than demonstration as it includes both substantiating and refuting. Both substantiation and argumentation are logical devices used to demonstrate the validity of a statement by other valid sentences.

The concepts used in the study are derived from the concepts of logical argumentation by F. H. van Eemeren *et al* (1996, pp. 7–8), according to which the conclusion is deduced from valid premises. Argumentation consists of complex speech acts aimed at solving a difference of opinions (Eemeren and Grootendorst, 1999, pp. 43).

The Structure of Argumentation

The article presents the quantitative data of the writers' argumentative skills revealed in the state exam compositions. There are two structures of argumentation given in the study materials: the SEC-category (Hennoste, 1998) and the SPEC-category (Kaldjärv, 2007).

The establishment of the structure of argumentation or the reasoning process following the SPEC-category (Statement, Premise or explanation, Example or argument and the Conclusion) is based on the approach described by the author in previously published materials (Kaldjärv, 2007).

The concept of the structure of argumentation (SPEC) has been developed in the course of the Estonian Debating Society activities since 1995. The debating methods of the Estonian Debating Society are based on a selection of works by US argumentation theorists, including Eric di Michele, a New York based debating instructor who worked as the methodological supervisor of American trainers while launching the debating movement in Eastern Europe. If at first the structure of argumentation in debating mainly included three components – statement, example and conclusion as the logical connection between the first two (SEC-category) – then soon the role and proportion of substantiation in argumentation increased considerably. The SPEC-category was completed at the turn of the millennium.

The structure of argumentation consists of complex speech acts fulfilling particular operations. They have a specific function in the structure. The statement or thesis is an opinion to be substantiated. In formulating the statement, a situation is described giving a context to the argumentation. The premise discusses the context further, gives more detailed basic concepts, values etc, and explains the extent to which various points of view coincide. The premise deduces the problem in the present situation; it gives a more detailed background to the context and provides the important starting point for substantiating the statement. The example or argument forms a significant part of the substantiation process. Arguments are logically connected with the premise(s) and the statement. The conclusion resolves and gives an evaluation to the argumentation.

Argumentative skills

Argumentative skills in the present study stand for the writer's structures of knowledge (based on the SPEC-category) that may be found and measured in the composition text. The argumentation in state exam compositions is explained and characterized by the following features: 1) the integrity of the substantiation, transitions, problem, the presentation of arguments and counterarguments in the whole composition, and 2) the comprehension of the function of the sub-thesis in the topic development with the respective discussion types on the paragraph level based on the flexible use of the SPEC-category. A crucial aspect in forming the discussion type is the presence of a premise in the structure, as it is with the premise that the problem based on the context is presented.

The structural logic of compositions has been the same in Estonia for decades: introduction, development of the topic, conclusion. This research was based on the principle that in order to prove the main statement made in the introduction, there must be sub-theses in the topic development and it is in the given sub-theses that the argumentation structure is employed at the paragraph level. There were no compositions in the total sample that would have only examples in the topic development. It may thus be concluded that it is in the topic development that sub-theses are presented and justified. The conclusions made in the topic development paragraphs must then be generalized in the conclusion so that it corresponds to the main statement or questions expressed in the introduction. Thus the SPEC-category can be applied in studies of argumentation at the text level as well as at the paragraph level. The use of argumentation structure (SPEC) at the various levels is justified as it enables the analysis of argumentation also in instances where components of the argumentation have been placed in the topic development paragraphs.

Method

The aim of this article is to explain the argumentation used in state exam compositions on the basis of quantitative research methods. In order to explain the implementation of the qualitative method, an analysis of the argumentation of one state exam composition is presented. In analyzing the argumentation in compositions, the qualitative values were encoded into quantitative ones. The level of measurement of the data analysis is the ratio level, differentiating the units of different value and ranking them according to allocated values. The present article focuses on the analysis of the occurrence of the features of argumentation structure in the text.

Sample

The population represented by the sample of the study includes the state exam compositions written in 1997, 2004–2006 and 2008. The main and total sample are differentiated in the research. The main sample includes the compositions written in 2004–2006 (altogether 1500 texts with 500 from each year); the total sample includes the state examinations written in 1997, 2004–2006, 2008 (altogether 1700 with further 100 compositions from 1997 and 2008). The total sample is used in the article to establish the discussion types, while the analysis of the argumentative skills is based on the main sample.

The study's total sample is used to group the state exam compositions written by secondary school students (16% from county center schools, 30% from city schools, 11% from schools with no catchment area, 25% from municipal or small town schools), vocational school students (6%) and adult secondary school students (12%) by school types. The number of compositions by secondary school students was the highest due to the fact that the state exam composition is only obligatory for secondary and adult secondary school students. The total sample included 773 men and 927 women (45% and 55% respectively). The state exam composition is written just prior to the completion of secondary school and the writers are mostly 18 years of age.

The largest group of the main sample consists of secondary school students (2004 – 411 students, 2005 – 429 students and 2006 – 382 students) which is coherent with the fact that writing the state exam composition is obligatory for graduates of both secondary and adult secondary schools (with 56 adult students writing it in 2004, 53 in 2005 and 77 in 2006), whereas vocational school students (33 students writing it in 2004, 18 in 2005 and 41 in 2006) have more freedom in selecting their state examinations. On the other hand, the vocational school students choosing the state exam composition are those who are motivated to continue their studies, as in order to enroll in a university they need to write a state exam composition requiring argumentation.

The implementation of the argumentation structure (SPEC) is considered on the basis of the whole of the composition. The composition's third paragraph is the second topic development paragraph, providing information to understand the substantiation of the main statement and to establish connections in the text.

The analysis of the argumentation in a state examination composition

In order to illustrate the qualitative method, a primary text of a state exam composition (2006, 356047) and an overview of the analysis of argumentation (Table 1) are presented.

Text sample "People who are difficult to understand" (2006, code 356047)

Para-graph	Text
1.	*1.1. Despite the similarities in appearance, every individual is unique and incomparable. 1.2. Further singularity is added by his soul and way of thinking. 1.3. It has nevertheless developed so that extremes do not fit into society. 1.4. Due to incomprehensibility, they are shunned. 1.5. Such people have, for instance, included thinkers and they have also been depicted in literature. 1.6. What is it that makes an individual incomprehensible to others?*
2.	*2.1. The ideas of the philosophers of the antiquity were so universal that they apply even today. 2.2. However, some of their thoughts were not as popular and comprehensible as they are today. 2.3. Plato did have his own school of followers, but apart from them his ideas were not extensively supported. 2.4. Instead, the philosopher's Allegory of the Cave and the theory of the soul being pulled by two horses have gained far more popularity today. 2.5. In the Allegory of the Cave Plato describes people seeing only shadows of the truth on the wall. 2.6. Only philosophers and intellectuals are able to look at the real light and get used to it. 2.7. Plato discussed the soul as a chariot pulled by two winged horses. 2.8. The soul yearns towards the edge of heaven behind which the truth may be seen. 2.9. However, one of the horses starts to buck thus pulling the chariot towards the sensual world. 2.10. Eventually the wings of the horses break, the soul falls without seeing the truth. 2.11. Plato's ideas seemed much too complicated and incomprehensible to the common people of his day as the discussion of the soul was still novel. 2.12. Therefore the philosopher's followers included only intellectuals. 2.13. This innovative way of thinking made Plato incomprehensible to other people.*
3.	*3.1. The ancient philosophies of life have found their supporters today. 3.2. Some of the teachings have even developed into religions. 3.3. Their full comprehension, however, requires patient concentration and attention that many lack. 3.4. Buddha's teachings have become increasingly popular in the Western world. 3.5. Nevertheless, there are only few ardent followers and people who understand it deeply. 3.6. The Dalai Lama has dedicated his life to meditation and the search for harmony in solitude. 3.7. He propagates the concept of peace and harmony in the world that can only be achieved by renouncing desires and wishes and accepting oneself. 3.8. Many find his ideas interesting but fail to reach their true content and understanding. 3.9. The English writer T.S. Eliot believes that it is the faraway Eastern culture that will come to save the Western world. 3.10 The statement finds confirmation in the seventh part "Fire Sermon" of his poem "The Waste Land". 3.11. According to the section, the war-torn West should look for support in Buddhism and peace that enables the understanding of the world. 3.12. Unfortunately only few people can follow, concentrate on and properly interpret the teachings of the Buddha and the Dalai Lama.*

Para- graph	Text
4	*4.1. The human soul is sometimes so restless that it cannot find support in religion or philosophy. 4.2. The individual is then directed by peculiar principles and understandings that may be incomprehensible to others. 4.3. Raskolnikov, the protagonist of F. Dostoyevsky's masterpiece "Crime and Punishment" followed his concept of dividing people into the important and the unimportant ones. 4.4. Trying to find confirmation of his theory, he decided to murder a usurer in order to foreground his own position. 4.5. The man's state of mind and behavior thereafter caused bewilderment in his family, in Sonia and Razumikhin. 4.6. Similarly, Raskolnikov's previously published article on his theory did not shed light on the situation. 4.7. The man's introversion and inner stress made him mysterious. 4.8. The writer R. Browning has said: "When the fight begins within himself, a man's worth something." 4.9. The innovative principles and theories of an individual may make him difficult to understand, but on the other hand also add to his peculiarity and individuality.*
5.	*5.1. The person's mystery may not always lie in inner conflicts. 5.2. By following solid convictions opposed to the present traditions one may appear highly enigmatic to others. 5.3. Timo, the character in J. Kross's "The Czar's Madman" was a person ahead of his time and the corresponding principles. 5.4. The man wanted to implement his ideas of equality and democracy. 5.5. According to Timo, people from different classes should have been equal. 5.6. Despite general disapproval he married a simple peasant girl. 5.7. However, the highly unconventional act for a Baltic German was justified, as the love between Timo and his wife lasted until death. 5.8. In the relatively stagnant and closed czarist country even the mere idea of democracy were unthinkable. 5.10. Therefore he sent his ruler a letter expressing his ideas of a more liberal order for the state. 5.11. The punishment included a long imprisonment, but even that could not break the man's beliefs. 5.12. However, his family and friends came to suspect Timo suffered from a mental disorder as his behavior was unthinkable within the contemporary norms. 5.13. The society was not yet mature enough for the man's ideals and thus could not think along with Timo's ideas.*
6.	*6.1. Instead of inability, the incomprehensibility may sometimes be caused by the wish not to see the truth. 6.2. However, there are some who also want to draw other people's attention to the reality.* *6.3. In most cases such people will not be heard and they are reprimanded as understanding them is difficult in the given situation. 6.4. The Russian writers A. Blok and A. Akhmatova criticized severely the revolution of early 20th century and its consequences. 6.5. Although A. Blok at first supported the reconstruction, he soon saw its devastating effect. 6.6. The following poetry expressed the despair and criticism related to the situation. 6.7. A. Akhmatova, however, criticized the younger generation for having been too naive to foresee and avoid the chaos. 6.8. The authorities shunned the texts of both writers and their work seemed to be futile. 6.9. But in his poem "Time" A. Alliksaar has said: "There are no futile times./ Their sense may not be revealed now." 6.10. So it happened also to these writers. 6.11. The poetry of Akhmatova and Blok gained popularity and their truth came to be understood only decades later when the nation's eyes had been opened after the mass psychosis.*

7.   *7.1. The inner world of a person is often incomprehensible even to himself. 7.2. An individual becomes incomprehensible to others due to his strenuous inner world and the peculiar or innovative philosophy which is not in keeping with the general convictions of the age. 7.3. The well-known writer O. Wilde has said: "Most people are other people. Their lives a mimicry, their passions a quotation." 7.4. There are only very few people who dare to think differently and express innovative ideas. 7.5. Thus, the exceptions should be all the more valued. 7.6. They are mostly criticized, however, it is precisely the people who are difficult to understand that may perceive the truth and perfect the world.*

The analysis of the argumentation of a state exam composition begins with the determination of the rhetoric features of the text: the composition text includes the introduction (paragraph 1), paragraphs of topic development (paragraphs 2–6) and the conclusion (paragraph 7).

Next, the structure of the composition text with regard to logic and dialectics is presented. The overview of the analysis of argumentation (Table 1) reveals how the writer presented his argumentation across the whole text.

Table 1 reveals how the main statement (1.3) is coherently connected with the sub-theses of the topic development (2.1, 3.1, 4.1, 5.1, 6.1) and developed into a generalization (7.6). The substantiation process of the composition has been logically opened in the topic development based on the structure of argumentation (SPEC). In the study, the compositions were analyzed with respect to macrostructures or topics and themes, with the formation of the macro speech acts or the abstract meaning of the higher text level. In the given state exam composition (2006, code 356047), the main statement, the sub-theses of the topic development and the generalization may be considered as macro speech acts. The writer has expressed the problem stemming from the context immediately after formulating the main statement in the introduction and after each sub-thesis in the topic development. From the dialectical point of view, the author of the text analyzed the arguments and counterarguments and formulated a conclusion in every paragraph. The transitions between the paragraphs are concise and the communicative principle functions. The given composition was analyzed according to the pragma-dialectical argumentation theory (Kaldjärv, 2011).

Table 1:   An overview of the argumentation in the state exam composition "People who are difficult to understand" (2006, code 356047)

Introduction
Main statement: *People with extremist views do not fit into the society.* (According to assertive 1.3) ↓ Premise: *Their views are not understood.* (Assertive 1.5.) *What makes an individual difficult to understand?* (Directive 1.6.) ↓

Development of the topic				
Sub-thesis: *The ideas of ancient philosophers still hold true today.* (Assertive 2.1)	Sub-thesis: *Ancient philosophies on life have their followers also today.* (Assertive 3.1)	Sub-thesis: *Sometimes people don't find support either in religion or philosophy.* (Assertive 4.1)	Sub-thesis: *The mystery of man is not always revealed in inner struggles.* (Assertive 5.1)	Sub-thesis: *Sometimes people do not want or wish to see the truth.* (Assertive 6.1)
Premise: *Plato's contemporaries found it hard to understand his ideas.*	Premise: *Understanding requires patient concentration and attention which many people lack.*	Premise: *Individuals are driven by their peculiar ideas and views which may remain incomprehensible to others.*	Premise: *There may be an opposition with the conventions of the given period.*	Premise: *In most cases they are ignored and discouraged as it is difficult to understand them in the given situation.*
Arguments: philosophers-intellectuals ↔ common people; present day	Arguments: Buddha's teachings, Dalai Lama, T. S. Eliot's "Waste Land" ↔ few understand	Arguments: Raskolnikov ↔ family, Sonia, Razumikhin; R. Browning	Arguments: Timo's ideas↔ Czar; family, acquaintances	Arguments: A. Blok, A. Akhmatova; A. Alliksaar ↔ Soviet power
Conclusion: *Intellectuals understood the innovative conceptual world.*	Conclusion: *Few can follow the teachings of Buddha and Dalai Lama, understand and interpret them correctly.*	Conclusion: *An individual's innovative principles may make him incomprehensible to others, but also add peculiar and unique features.*	Conclusion: *Society did not understand his ideals.*	Conclusion: *The poetry of Akhmatova and Blok gained popularity and their truth was understood only decades later when people's eyes were opened from the mass psychosis.*

↓
Conclusion, generalization People who are difficult to understand may know the truth and perfect the world. (Assertive 7.6)

The writer of state exam composition is free in his choices. Based on the total sample of the doctoral thesis, it may be stated that the writers mostly used the SPE-category. In other words, the students did not reach the conclusion on the paragraph level of the composition. However, while the SPEC-category may have occurred in one of the composition's other paragraphs, the number of compositions with a coherent connection between all paragraphs was small. The comprehension of a text is more complicated if the writer's train of thought has been distributed episodically in the topic development so that the conclusion may have been presumed only on the basis of several paragraphs. It may be stated on the basis of the study results that due to the lack of the components of the structure of argumentation, the abundance of descriptions and narrations and the sporadic elementary speech acts, many of the compositions were merely a sequence of interruptions.

This article presents the data of the application of the argumentation structure on the paragraph and text level of the state exam compositions in 2004–2006, followed by the analysis of the differences between male and female students from different school types. Then the discussion types based on the third paragraph of the compositions are presented establishing the five most widely used argumentation types. The discussion types are based on the argumentation structure (SPEC-category) and the problem-solving (SPRE – situation, problem, response, evaluation) approach by M. Hoey (1979). The SPEC-category forms the basic structure the components of which enable the determination of other discussion types used in the composition texts.

Results

The data analysis first presents the results of the argumentation structure implementation, then concentrates on the argumentative skills by gender and school type and highlights the statistically significant differences.

The Argumentation in State Exam Compositions by School Type

The focus on one paragraph in the composition is important in order to explain students' understanding of the connection between the idea of the sub-thesis and the main statement.

The results of the argumentative skills in 2004–2006 are given in Figure 1. The column entitled "3rd paragraph" marks the use of the full argumentation structure (SPEC) in the third paragraph of the composition and "The whole text" respectively the use of argumentation structure across the whole text.

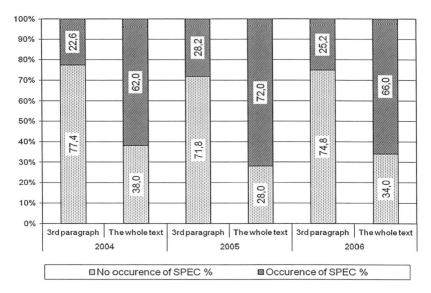

Figure 1: *The occurrence of the full argumentation structure (SPEC) in the third paragraph and the whole text of the state exam compositions (in %) in 2004–2006.*

It may be concluded on the basis of Figure 1 that the use of the full argumentation structure on the third paragraph level is equally low for all students in the main sample: 2004 – 22.6%, 2005 – 28.2% and 2006 – 25.2%. However, considering all the paragraphs of the text, more instances of the full argumentation structure may be found: 2004 – 62%, 2005 – 72% and 2006 – 66% of the students of the main sample use the SPEC-category. The use of the full argumentation structure (SPEC) in state exam compositions has slightly increased over the years. The best results in argumentation on the paragraph and text level date back to 2005. The difference over the years is not considerable, however. Therefore in order to determine the situation in detail, we first focus on the various school types and then the argumentative skills of male and female students.

Table 2 presents the data of the implementation of SPEC-category in the compositions by students from different school types in 2004–2006. The higher results in the argumentation of the third paragraph and the whole text in 2005 may be explained by the proportion of the students from a specific school type: compared to other years, the number of secondary school students was the highest (429 students) and the number of vocational school students (18) and adult secondary school students (53) respectively the lowest. The number of vocational school and adult secondary school students writing the composition in the sample increased considerably in 2006.

Table 2: *The occurrence of SPEC-category in the third paragraph and the whole text by school types over the years*

			Year					
			2004		2005		2006	
School type			3rd paragraph	The whole text	3rd paragraph	The whole text	3rd paragraph	The whole text
Secondary school	Occurrence	N	104	274	127	324	108	277
		%	25.3	66.7	29.6	75.5	28.3	72;5
	Total	N	411	411	429	429	382	382
Vocational school	Occurrence	N	3	10	3	8	3	16
		%	9.1	30.3	16.7	44.4	7.3	39
	Total	N	33	33	18	18	41	41
Adult secondary school	Occurrence	N	6	26	11	28	15	37
		%	10.7	46.4	20.8	52.8	19.5	48.1
	Total	N	56	56	53	53	77	77

The data presented in Table 2 show that the argumentative skills of secondary school students were better than those of vocational and adult secondary school students. Although the number of vocational and adult secondary school students writing the state exam composition was smaller than those from secondary schools, it was important to also emphasize the argumentative skills of students of the given school types. However, secondary school students were similarly in need of improvement.

The argumentation of the third paragraph in the compositions of adult secondary school students has exhibited some increase with the best result from 2005 (20.8% of the adult secondary school students using the argumentation structure). Compared to other years, the best results in the argumentation of the whole text by adult secondary school students once again date back to 2005 (52.8%).

The argumentation of the third paragraph in the compositions of vocational school students was inconsistent: the best results were featured in 2005 (16.7% of the vocational school students using the full argumentation structure), but the results from 2006 were even lower than the results from 2004. Although there has been some increase in the argumentation of the whole text, the results from 2005 were somewhat better than the results of other years (44.4% of vocational school students in 2005).

The samples of students from adult secondary and vocational schools were very small and thus the results cannot be considered as showing generalizable tendencies. The fluctuation may be dependent on the individual features of the sample of the given year.

However, we may state on the basis of the results that the argumentative skills of secondary school students were better than those of other school types. The reasons were probably due to the fact that the number of Estonian language lessons was higher in the secondary school and therefore more time was devoted to discussion and argumentation. The problems seem to be severest in the argumentative skills of vocational school students. On the other hand, the aims of the learning outcomes in the curriculum were the same for all school types and thus it was important to analyze the use of language in argumentation by the students of different school types.

Tests of significance by school type and gender

In the following, chi-square tests were used to compare the occurrence of the SPEC-category in the third paragraph of the state exam compositions over the years 2004–2006 by school types (Table 3).

Table 3: *The change in the use of full argumentation structure in the third paragraph in years 2004–2006 by school types*

School type	N	χ^2	Significance probability
Secondary school	1222	2.014(a)	0.365
Vocational school	92	1.267(b)	0.531
Adult secondary school	186	2.405(c)	0.300

The reader can see in Table 3 that there were no statistically significant changes in the third paragraph argumentation over the years 2004–2006 for secondary school, adult secondary school as well as for vocational school students.

An overview is given of the discussion types based on the third paragraph of the state exam compositions of the total sample. The argumentation structure (SPEC-category) forms the basis of the establishment of the discussion type. As the problem constitutes a mandatory component of the argumentative text type (Lepajõe, 2002, pp. 271), its closest equivalent in the argumentation structure is the premise. In formulating the premise, the collated circumstances were given as the background information that highlights the logically valid premises in the argumentation followed by the appropriate examples or reasons to substantiate the statement. In state exam compositions students mainly express the problem by using an interrogative sentence when presenting the circumstances related to the premise.

When limiting the discussion types to the five most frequently used categories, we get the following discussion types presented in Figure 2.

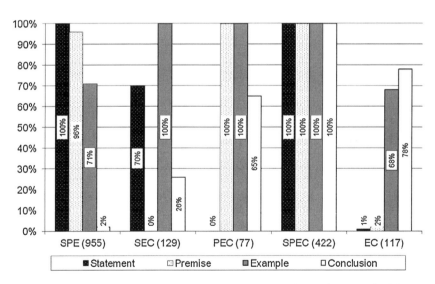

Figure 2: *The most frequently used discussion types based on the third paragraph of the state exam compositions of the total sample (bars represent the proportion of the compositions in the group where particular structural element is present)*

Although previously published materials (Hennoste, 1998; Kaldjärv, 2007) describe only two types of the argumentation structure, it may be concluded from the analysis of the state exam compositions that students use various paragraph construction techniques. Table 4 describes the most widely used discussion types over the studied years.

Table 4:   *The most widely used discussion types in the third paragraph of the full sample*

Discussion types		Year				
		1997	2004	2005	2006	2008
SPE (955)	N	64	289	269	277	56
	%	64.0	57.8	53.8	55.4	56.0
SPEC (422)	N	22	112	140	127	21
	%	22.0	22.4	28.0	25.4	21.0
SEC (129)	N	4	52	40	21	12
	%	4.0	10.4	8.0	4.2	12.0
EC (117)	N	10	43	32	22	10
	%	10.0	8.6	6.4	4.4	10.0
PEC (77)	N		4	19	53	1
	%		0.8	3.8	10.6	1.0
Total	N	100	500	500	500	100
	%	100.0	100.0	100.0	100.0	100.0

According to Table 4, students mostly use the SPE-type. In using the SPE-type in their state exam composition, students do not word the conclusion of their argument in the third paragraph of the topic development. The SPEC (Kaldjärv, 2007) was the second most widely used category. The third most common type was SEC (Hennoste, 1998). It is worth pointing out in Figure 2 that the role of the conclusion in the SEC-type was minimal, and thus the result could rather be named SE-type. The EC-type was the fourth and PEC the fifth. The element of the problem typical of the argumentative text type that students mostly express as the circumstances in the premise was featured in categories SPE, PEC and SPEC. Types SEC and EC do not contain the presumed circumstances that would feature the problem.

Next the occurrence of the argumentation structure in the other paragraphs of the composition was considered. If the writer distributed the argumentation structure across several paragraphs, it was considered with reference to descriptive data analysis. The same applied to sections composed on the basis of narrative, defining and other principles. Paragraph structures that did not comply with the argumentation structure were excluded from the present study.

The argumentation in the state exam composition as a whole text is somewhat better than argumentation in the third paragraph, meaning that the full argumentation structure (SPEC) may occur in some other paragraph of the state exam composition. The argumentation in the whole text means the analysis of the argumentation across all the paragraphs. The differences in the argumentation of the whole text occurring in the compositions of the main sample of different school types over the years are given in Table 5.

Table 5: *The change in the use of full argumentation structure across the whole text in years 2004–2006 by school types*

School type	N	χ^2	Significance probability
Secondary school	1222	8.326(a)	0.016
Vocational school	92	1.135(b)	0.567
Adult secondary school	186	0.487(c)	0.784

It is seen that the occurrence of the full argumentation structure (SPEC) in the whole text has a statistically significant difference between years 2004–2006 in the compositions by the main sample secondary school students. However, there were no statistically significant differences in the argumentation of the whole text by vocational school students (p=0.567) and adult secondary school students (p=0.784).

Next we compared the argumentative skills of the students from different school types by year and gender (Table 6). Table 6 shows that in all years for both male and female students there were statistically significant differences between students from different school types in the use of the full argumentation structure (SPEC) in the whole text (in all subgroups p<0.05).

Table 6:   *The occurrence of SPEC-category across the whole text for students from different*
school types by gender and year of the exam

The occurrence of SPEC-category across the whole text			School type			N	χ^2	P
			Secondary school	Vocational school	Adult secondary school			
2004	men	Occurrence of SPEC	62.60%	30.40%	34.80%	124	13.433	0.001
	women	Occurrence of SPEC	69.60%	30.00%	54.50%	186	9.123	0.01
2005	men	Occurrence of SPEC	68.40%	45.50%	45.50%	132	6.389	0.041
	women	Occurrence of SPEC	80.20%	42.90%	58.10%	228	12.416	0.002
2006	men	Occurrence of SPEC	76.10%	45.80%	51.20%	172	16.424	0
	women	Occurrence of SPEC	69.20%	29.40%	44.40%	158	16.792	0

Some improvement of the argumentative skills among the main sample over the
years is illustrated in Figure 3 describing the proportional occurrence of
argumentation among men and women both in the third paragraph and in the
whole text in 2004–2006.

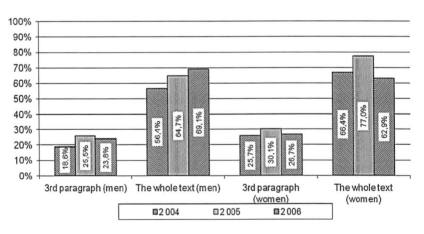

Figure 3:   *The occurrence of SPEC-category in the third paragraph and the whole text of the*
composition by gender in 2004–2006

It may be concluded from Figure 3 that while the argumentative skills of men across the whole text have somewhat improved over the years, women's argumentation is inconsistent. On the other hand, in 2006 men's argumentative skills across the whole text were better than those of women. In addition to the structure of the composition paragraphs, the transitions between the paragraphs play a significant role in argumentation. The final sentence of the topic development paragraph and the first sentence of the following paragraph form the transition between the paragraphs (Mäger, 1993). M. Hennoste (1998) has named the given sentences as core sentences. In the argumentation structure equivalent functions are carried by statements and conclusions.

An overview of the use of transitions in state exam compositions in 2004–2006 is given in Table 6, with transitions and connections between the paragraphs on the basis of argumentation from the introduction to the conclusion organized by school type. The row headed "No occurrence" denotes a situation where the paragraphs of the state exam composition were not connected to each other and there was no substantiation based on the main statement in the text. The row headed "Occasional occurrence" means that at least half of the state exam composition had been coherently connected. The row headed "Frequent occurrence" means that more than half or the whole of the exam composition had been coherently structured. Table 7 presents the results of the main sample of the argumentation from the main statement to the conclusion and the transitions in their state exam compositions.

The use of argumentation from the main statement to the conclusion and the transitions between the paragraphs of state exam compositions by students from the various school types differs significantly (p<0.01). Exam composition writers from all different school types have difficulties in forming a coherently unified text. 20.7% of the secondary school students of the main sample can prove the main statement expressed in the introduction and implement the transitions systematically, and respectively 5.4% of the vocational school students and 6.5% adult secondary school students of the sample.

Table 7:   *Argumentation from the main statement to the conclusion and the transitions in*
           state exam compositions by school type in 2004–2006

Crosstab					
Transitions		School type			Total
		Secondary school	Vocational school	Adult secondary school	
No occurrence	Count	25	10	12	47
	% within school type	2.0%	10.9%	6.5%	3.1%
Occasional occurrence	Count	944	77	162	1183
	% within school type	77.3%	83.7%	87.1%	78.9%
Frequent occurrence	Count	253	5	12	270
	% within school type	20.7%	5.4%	6.5%	18.0%
Total	Count	1222	92	186	1500
	% within school type	100.0%	100.0%	100.0%	100.0%

Discussion and Conclusion

The present article discusses the use of the argumentation structure (SPEC) in
the state examination compositions. The results presented in the article confirm
that there were differences in the argumentation of the state exam compositions
by gender and school types.

The study shows that students select various methods to structure their
argumentation in the state exam compositions. Comparing the various
approaches to argumentation, we see that in their argumentation in state exam
compositions students tend to prefer some form of the SPEC-category which
was also the basis of the research. The results have shown that the selected
structure was well founded. The SPEC-category can be implemented in various
manners: using the argumentation structure in a paragraph (with five to nine
sentences as the average paragraph length), but also when distributing the
argumentation across several paragraphs. The main problem seems to be that the
paragraph which is supposed to carry one idea is not coherent in content and
thus the comprehensibility of the whole text suffers.

In developing argumentation in the state exam compositions, the most
frequently selected discussion type by students is SPE. This means that students
have made their choice and left out the generalized conclusion of their

argumentation. In his textbook "Kirjutamise kunst" (The Art of Writing), M. Ehala (2000, pp. 71) states that in analyzing the content paragraph it is important to find the core idea which is expressed by the core sentence (statement or conclusion). According to M. Ehala, the core sentence may be positioned at the beginning or the end of the paragraph or remain unexpressed in words if it is clear from the paragraph. In the same textbook the author also adds that one "should be careful with paragraphs without the core sentence".

In the content paragraph of the topic development, the student has to substantiate the validity of the example and logically connect the previously presented premises. However, if the writer develops the argumentation to the conclusion himself, it is easier for the reader to understand the text. This has become increasingly important at present as texts have shortened.

The discussion types show that the problem (in state exam compositions usually near the premise) occurs only in three types (SPE, PEC, SPEC), and thus the element of the problem must also be stressed in the learning process. The role of the problem in composition writing will increase in the future, since as of 2012 everyone who takes and passes the exam needs to find a problem on the basis of the given text and write a relevant problem-centered composition. Therefore, understanding the argumentation structure (SPEC) and relating it to the problem-solving approach by M. Hoey (1979) characterizing the argumentative text type is of utmost importance.

There were differences in the argumentation of state exam compositions by gender and school types. The study results presented in the article show that the SPEC-category was best used in the third paragraph and the whole text by secondary school students. The use of the full argumentation structure in state exam composition by the vocational and adult secondary school students was less frequent. Although one can question the necessity of using the full argumentation structure at the paragraph level, the author is convinced that the whole text (be it 400 or 600–800 words in the future) will improve if the writer has a better understanding of the function of the main statement in the argumentation.

Students choose their style of writing and manner of discussion on the basis of their knowledge and experience. If the main statement in the introduction is not developed further in the topic development paragraphs, the fundamental idea of the composition will change or disappear. The analysis of the transitions of the introduction, topic development paragraphs and the conclusion of the state exam compositions shows that students sometimes lack the skill of making the text a coherent whole and developing the main statement to the conclusion. In order to improve the argumentative skills, it is important to work more on the paragraph and only then on the whole text.

The changes introduced in the organization of the state examination composition in 2012 require the students to have a better understanding of argumentation. The present study explains the choices made in the argumentation of the state exam compositions during the previous form of the exam.

References

Austin, J. L. (1962). *How to do things with words.* Oxford: Clarendon Press.

Ehala, M. (2000). *Kirjutamise kunst.* [The Art of Writing.] Tallinn: Künnimees (in Estonian).

Grauberg, E. (1996). *Loogika, keel ja mõtlemine.* [Logic, language and thinking.] Tallinn: Tallinna Bakalaureuse Erakool (in Estonian).

Dijk, T. A. van (1980). Macrostructures: An interdisciplinary study of global structures in discourse. *Interaction and cognition.* Hillsdale, N. J.: L. Erlbaum Associates.

Eemeren, F. H. van, Grootendorst, R. (1992). *Argumentation, communication and fallacies: A pragma-dialectical perspective.* New Jersey: Lawrence Erlbaum Associates.

Eemeren, F. H. van, Grootendorst, R., Snoeck Henkemans, F., Blair, J. A., Johnson, R. H., Krabbe, E. C. W., Plantin, C., Walton, D. N., Willard, C. A., Woods, J., Zarefsky, D. (1996). *Fundamentals of argumentation theory: A handbook of historical backgrounds and contemporary developments.* New Jersey: Lawrence Erlbaum Associates.

Eemeren, F. H. van, & Grootendorst, R. (1999). Developments in argumentation theory. In J. Andriessen, & P. Coirier (Eds.). *Foundations of argumentative text processing,* (pp. 43–58). Amsterdam: Amsterdam University Press.

Eemeren, F. H. van, & Grootendorst, R. (2004). *A Systematic theory of argumentation: The pragma-dialectic approach.* Cambridge: University Press.

Grice, P. (1975). Logic and conversation. In P. Cole & J. Morgan (Eds.). *Syntax and semantixs.* (*Volume 3: Speech acts,* pp. 41–58). New York: Academic Press.

Grice, P. (1989). *Studies in the way of words.* Cambridge, Massachusetts – London: Harvard University Press.

Hennoste, M. (1998). *Arukas arutleja.* [A sensible arguer.] Tallinn: Virgela (in Estonian).

Hennoste, M. (2005). Eesti keele riigieksami arendamise vajadusest: probleeme ja lahendusi. [The need for the development of the Estonian language state examination: Problems and solutions] In M. Kadakas (Ed.). *Eesti keele ja kirjanduse õpetamisest koolis,* (pp. 76–79). Tallinn: Argo (in Estonian).

Hoey, M. (1979). *Signalling in discourse: Discourse analysis monographs 6.* English Language Research. Birmingham: University of Birmingham.

Hoey, M. (Ed.) (1994). Signalling in discourse: a functional analysis of a common discourse pattern in written and spoken English. *Advances in written text analysis,* 26–45. London: Routledge.

Hoey, M. (2001). *Textual interaction: An introduction to written discourse analysis.* London: Routledge.

Kaldjärv, M. (2007). *Argumendi jõud.* [The force of the argument.] Tallinn: Koolibri (in Estonian.).

Kaldjärv, M. (2011). Pragma-dialectics on the basis of state examination compositions. In V. Lamanauskas, (Ed.). *Problems of education in the 21st century: Current tendencies and problems in education, 38,* pp. 37–49.

Krippendorf, K. (1980). *Content analysis: An introduction to its methodology.* Beverly Hills CA: Sage.

Lepajõe, K. (2002). Argumenteerimisoskusest eksamikirjandite põhjal. [On argumentative skills on the basis of exam compositions] *Keel ja Kirjandus, 4,* pp. 269–274 (in Estonian).

Levinson, S. (1983). *Pragmatics.* Cambridge University Press.

Mey, J. (2001). *Pragmatics: An introduction.* Oxford: Blackwell Publishers.

Mäger, M. (1993). *Eesti keele õpik 12.klassile.* [Estonian language study book for year 12] Tallinn: Koolibri (in Estonian).

Rehg, W. (2001). *Lecture: The argumentation theorist in deliberative democracy.* International Debate Education Association. Prague, October 13, 2001.

Searle, J. R. (1969). *Speech acts: An essay in the philosophy of language.* Cambridge: Cambridge University Press.

Vuks, G. (1999). *Traditsiooniline formaalne loogika.* [Traditional formal logic.] Tartu: Sihtasutus Iuridicum (in Estonian).

Õim, H. (1986). Pragmaatika ja keelelise suhtlemise teooria. [Pragmatics and the theory of verbal communication.] *Keel ja Kirjandus, 5,* pp. 257–269 (in Estonian).

Estonian Studies in Education

Edited by Jaan Mikk, Marika Veisson and Piret Luik

www.peterlang.com